4 SUPER POWERS

DISCOVER THE
EXTRAORDINARY
IN YOU

Ipomea Chaudhary

Clever Fox® PUBLISHING
Chennai • Bangalore

CLEVER FOX PUBLISHING
Chennai, India

Published by CLEVER FOX PUBLISHING 2026

ISBN: 978-93-7500-960-3

Introduction

Before your feet touch the ground in the morning, your mind has already travelled far away from you. You have scrolled through lives you are not living. Absorbed opinions you did not ask for. Felt pressures you did not consciously choose. And somewhere in that quiet process, you moved a little further away from yourself.

We are the most connected generation in history. And yet, many people feel deeply alone. We have access to unlimited knowledge yet remain unsure of our own direction. We are constantly improving ourselves, but rarely stopping to ask one simple question: Who am I becoming—and is it truly me? Beneath this question lies a deeper, unspoken fear. A fear of being left behind.

Artificial Intelligence is learning faster than we are. Jobs that once promised lifelong security are disappearing. Entire industries are reshaping themselves overnight. People are not just questioning their careers. They are questioning their value. What if I am no longer needed?

What if I am replaceable? What if everything I built my identity around can vanish? For the first time in human history, humanity is confronting its own creation—and wondering where it stands.

What is the role of humanity in all this?

If we are the creators, why do we feel so powerless?

Why do we trust science, barely older than our civilizations, while dismissing the ancient intelligence of intuition?

Why do religions—born from shared truths—become tools of division?

This book was born from those questions.

It is not a manual for success, nor a shortcut to wealth. A mirror held gently to help you rediscover the superpowers you already carry—powers buried under conditioning, performance, and the noise of modern life. Powers that transcend algorithms, trends, and metrics.

In my work as a healer, therapist, and coach, I have worked with people at their most vulnerable. People who, from the outside, appeared successful, capable, and in control— inside felt anxious, disconnected, or unsure of their place in the world. Exhausted from trying to be enough—professionals chasing impossible standards, women dissolving themselves for others, young adults torn between curated identities, and those battling emotional and physical illnesses.

I began to see a pattern. Their suffering was not a lack of intelligence, talent, or opportunity. It was a loss of connection to their inner authority. They had learned how to function—but had forgotten how to trust themselves. We are living in a time of immense external advancement, but very little inner awareness.

We are taught how to achieve, but not how to remain steady in uncertainty.

This book is needed now because the world is changing faster than ever before. Roles, identities, and systems that once gave people certainty are shifting. And in the absence of external certainty, the only stable ground left is internal. This is where the real superpowers live.

My own journey began when I left a thriving media career to raise my children. What felt like a pause from the outside became an opening within. I turned to yoga and energy work, Pranic Healing, Arhatic Yoga and Clinical Hypnotherapy. Each step revealed more of who I truly was.

Every person already carries within them the ability to heal, to transform, and to rise beyond their conditioning. They do not need to be given power. They need to remember it. This book is my contribution to that remembering.

I have stood at the crossroads of science, spirituality, theosophy, and philosophy—each offering a piece of the human puzzle. Science gave precision. Spirituality revealed the unseen. Theosophy connected me to ancient wisdom. Philosophy taught me to question everything. Together, they illuminated a deeper truth. Through meditation and inner work, I experienced moments of clarity that felt less like learning and more like remembering.

This book is for those who feel caught between who they are and who they are expected to be. For those ready to reclaim their inner truth and walk through life with courage.

Real superpowers are not loud. They reveal themselves through quiet courage, compassion, and clarity—often overlooked in a world that values visibility over depth.

In Egypt, standing before the Sphinx, I saw this truth reflected in symbol. The human head, the strength of the bull, the courage of the lion, and the vision of the eagle—together representing the awakened human. To become the Sphinx is to unlearn, remember, and awaken the powers within.

This book is not mine. The truths it holds have always existed. My role is simply to remind you of what you already know. The original meaning of education—*educare*—was to draw out what lies within. It's time we return to that.

By the time you finish this book, I hope you will:

- See yourself differently
- Feel that you can do anything
- Act boldly
- Inspire others

The future doesn't depend on how fast we move ahead of each other or our machines. It depends on how deeply we remember what it means to be human.

The future will not belong to the most intelligent machines.

It will belong to the most awakened humans.

Acknowledgements

This book is the result of many influences, sacred guidance, and unwavering support from those who have shaped my understanding of what it means to awaken our superpowers.

To my beloved family—your love, patience, and encouragement have been the foundation upon which this work stands. To my husband, thank you for holding the fort with quiet strength and unwavering faith. Your presence has been my anchor. To my children, thank you for choosing me. Your existence is the greatest divine gift, and your light continues to inspire my journey.

I offer this book in deep reverence to my Grand Master Choa Kok Sui. His teachings in Pranic Healing and Arhatic Yoga have illuminated my path with clarity, purpose, and grace. His wisdom continues to guide me toward a life of healing, self-discovery, and service—one that is intensely extraordinary.

To all my teachers—both seen and unseen—I bow in gratitude. I acknowledge the timeless wisdom and blessings of Shri Yukteshwar Giri, Paramhansa Yoganandaji, Sri Ramana Maharishi, J Krishnamurthy and the lineage of Masters of Theosophy. The compassionate philosophy of His Holiness the Dalai Lama, and the pioneering insights of Dr Bruce Lipton, Dr Richard Davidson, Dr Kristin Neff, and many others have helped bridge the realms of science and spirit, bringing depth and validation to this work. I thank Shyam Nair for his editorial expertise and research assistance.

This book is a tribute to the limitless potential of the human spirit. It is an offering to those who have walked before me, those who walk beside me now, and those who will continue this journey of awakening and service.

With deepest gratitude, respect and love.

Contents

The First Super Power

GRATITUDE

The Unseen Gift

Imagine swimming in an ocean of abundance where everything is right in front of us. Immersed in this boundless space of fortune, love, opportunities, resources, and yet being unaware of this reality. That's exactly what many of us do! We drudge along, waiting for luck, better times, or outside help. The pressures of a mundane daily life consume our attention. This distracts us from noticing the possibilities that exist beyond our immediate concerns.

The password to move from our current reality to unlocking our immense dormant potential is nothing else than the superpower of Gratitude. Do not underestimate the latent capability of this gentle giant! It can effortlessly move mountains if harnessed the right way.

The practice of gratitude goes beyond saying a common 'Thank you', a phrase that has taken the role of the most favourite social formality- a polite request or tick mark in the box of good manners. Thanks is perceived as a transaction, emphasising the fact that you did something for me, so I say thank you to maintain the social interaction.

Often, parents prompt children to say it as part of 'good manners', and sometimes, more to just reassure themselves that they are raising good children, and they are good parents. But, thank you is not about the words, rather the energy behind them.

When expressed with a genuine meaning of gratitude, it creates a real connection. It acknowledges effort, presence, and humanity.

The word Gratitude can be derived from the Latin word 'Gratus', which means 'Thankful' or 'Pleasing'. It can also be derived from 'Gratia', which means 'Grace', 'Graciousness', or 'Gratefulness'. The deeper layers in the quality of gratitude reflect in accepting the grace of a higher power, love as kindness and generosity as mercy. The qualities of love, kindness, generosity, mercy, and grace are codes of conduct mentioned in every culture around the world. Gratitude is the bedrock on which most religions are formed.

The echo of this powerful quality can be felt in salutations such as a 'Namaste', where both hands are placed together to greet or in respect and reverence. Namaste is a combination of two words: 'Namah', which means 'bow' and 'te', which means you. Hence, the deeper meaning here is that 'The divine in me bows down in respect to the divine in you'. Joining the palms is called the Anjali mudra in the ancient science of yoga. This is done in front of the heart. Both palms press each other, activating the nerve endings on the finger tips; these pressure points further activate the brain. There is also a connection between this mudra and stress relief, as well as the feeling of happiness. It also aids in enhancing a deeper connection with people.

A Spiritual Perspective

In Christianity, gratitude is connected to the concept of grace, God's unmerited favour towards humanity. The foundation of Christian gratitude rests on the idea that everything believers receive comes from God's generous love, particularly the gift of salvation. This understanding transforms gratitude from just a practice of politeness into a profound spiritual virtue.

"For everything God created is good, and nothing is to be rejected if it is received with thanksgiving, because it is consecrated by the word of God and prayer."

– 1 Timothy 4:4-5, Bible

The Hindu faith identifies gratitude through the Sanskrit term kṛitajna (कृतज्ञ), meaning "one who recognises all favours done". Hindu philosophy considers ingratitude (kṛitaghna) among the gravest sins, declaring "there is no expiation for the ungrateful one".

Most Hindu prayers pay an ode of gratitude to various deities and the aspect of energy they represent. For instance, Hanuman represents faith, protection and eternal love - "OM Hanumate namah". Shiva represents will power- "Om Namah Shivaya". Ganesha represents wisdom, knowledge and the eternal obstacle remover- "OM Ganeshaya namah".

In Islam, gratitude is a duty towards God and all his blessings. Thankfulness is described in three ways: 1. To realise the blessings in the heart 2. To say thanks with the tongue 3. To express gratitude in action by doing righteous deeds.

Amongst many, chapter 4, verse 147 of the Quran asks-"Why should God make you suffer torment if you are thankful and believe in him? God always rewards gratitude, and He knows everything."

Gratitude is a core part of humanity's cultural festivities. Come autumn, and the western part of the world celebrates "Thanksgiving". This annual tradition of celebrating harvest signifies respect for ancestors, reaping the benefits of the past, and sowing new seeds of gratitude with loved ones. It honours the providence and abundance of good deeds.

In India, winter ushers in the advent of "Lohri" in Punjab, "Pongal" in Tamil Nadu and "Bohali Bihu" in Assam, all unique celebrations of harvest. The rains bring in the time to celebrate Onam in Kerala, the southern state's official harvest festival.

Harvest festivals are a way to express gratitude to nature, the earth and deities of abundance and seasonal cycles. Nature is an unconditional giver. Food, air, and water sustain us. These rituals help humans connect with nature, the source of human sustenance.

The significance of rituals around giving thanks in various cultures, such as Thanksgiving, Harvest festivals, Diwali or Eid, is to concretise the attribute of gratitude so that it is carried forward as a tradition to future generations.

The inherent beauty of Gratitude can be seen in the timeless tale of Krishna, Pandavas, Durvasa Rishi and a grain of rice. In the legend of the Mahabharata, during the exile of the Pandavas, Rishi Durvasa announced he would visit them in the forest with his disciples for a meal. Known for an extremely short temper, Rishi Durvasa was infamous for his practice of shooting curses in a state of anger.

As luck would have it, the sage arrived when the Pandavas and Draupadi had finished eating, and thus, there was no food left. Draupadi panicked at the thought of Rishi Durvasa's anger and a possible curse. Stuck in despair, she invoked the name of Lord Krishna with full faith. Krishna appeared, in his cool sense of all-knowing, and asked for something to eat. Draupadi was already afraid and distraught, but the Lord asked for just an empty pot of food. Examining it carefully, he found a grain of rice. He thanked Draupadi for the food and ate the tiny grain of rice, which satisfied his hunger. Soon after, Rishi Durvasa surprisingly felt satiated, blessed the Pandavas and Draupadi, and left.

There are multiple layers of lessons in this story. At a deeper level, Krishna symbolises higher consciousness, Pandavas represent the energy centres of the subtle body called the Chakras, and Draupadi embodies the powerful central meridian called the Shushumna Nadi. Rishi Durvasa represents the lower vibrational emotion of anger, and his disciples are the many shades of anger, such as irritation, rage, and annoyance.

When you end up in a situation that can unleash your anger or trigger someone else's anger issues, one of the ways out is not to react and avoid getting entangled in drama. Instead, one could wilfully embrace the spirit of gratitude. When we invoke higher consciousness with faith and no doubt, it fills us with enough gratitude to swim through the anger.

The above story also touches upon Draupadi's earthen pot, which is always brimming with food. This underlines the organic correlation between abundance, gratitude and giving without fear.

Similarly, one of Christianity's most famous psalms is, "You prepare a table before me in the presence of my enemies; you anoint my head with oil; my cup runs over"- Psalm 23:5. This verse guides us during the most difficult times in our lives by helping us count the blessings we have, and reminding us our cup will never be empty. Just like that one grain in Draupadi's pot which satiated Krishna, Durvasa Rishi and his disciples. The word "Enemies" in the psalm refers to one's own self-limiting, self- depreciating, lowering thoughts and feelings which focus on fears, doubts and what we do not have.

The abundant and overflowing nature of blessings and mercy can be unlocked with the appreciation of all things available to us already. The modern version of this rhetoric is the phrase "Is your cup half empty, or half full?" Pessimists will look at the cup half empty and try to fill it with what is not there. The glass is the same; it is about the perception of the observer. The quality of the perception is the enemy within.

At the end of the day, gratitude only comes with humility. J Krishnamurthy advocated humility to be the act of seeing things as they are without distortion, biases, judgment, or comparison.

This state of heightened awareness fosters truthfulness, openness and authenticity.

Humility is a powerful weapon that can calmly disarm a potentially volatile person or situation without much effort and destruction. It may often be looked at as an antidote to excessive pride; however, that is only when one is trying to be humble for the external trappings of this virtue. Humility cannot be cultivated. It can only come with dropping all conditioning and not holding value in achievements. Pride in achievements is a potential self-destructive weapon which hampers personal growth and evolution.

When Control Misleads

"The best soldiers are not warlike; the best fighters do not lose their temper. The greatest conquerors are those who overcome their enemies without strife. The greatest directors of men are those who yield place to others. This is called the Virtue of not striving, the capacity for directing mankind; this is being the compeer of Heaven. It was the highest goal of the ancients."

– Lao Tsu

Humans tend to overestimate their control over events and outcomes. The illusion of control is more of a psychological defence mechanism that helps them feel confident and secure in their abilities to navigate uncertainties. The innate desire to control provides an illusion of power. There are many factors leading to this distortion of truth.

One of the best ways to understand this further is through studying The Dunning Kruger. This research states that we end up treating favourable outcomes as self-produced to maintain confidence and hope in the face of uncertainty. The Dunning Krugger effect could potentially play a role in individuals' tendency to overestimate their control over their lives due to cognitive biases.

Then comes the "Illusion of separation," which can potentially contribute to a lack of realisation that humans are interconnected with the world around them. We tend to inhabit a pattern of attributing our successes to skill and hard work, while failures are blamed on bad luck or the external environment.

Recognising and working with our external environment requires a shift towards systems thinking or the "Systems Approach", a concept that views complex systems as an interdependent whole rather than isolated parts. This perspective encourages people to consider the broader context of their choices and situations, leading to the awareness of feedback loops where actions lead to consequences. These feedback loops have a lasting long-term impact on behaviours and decisions.

Systems are dynamic and non-linear, with multiple interacting variables that can lead to unpredictable outcomes. Hence, attempts to control and predict outcomes may be futile. Therefore, always look at the larger picture and identify those minute leverage points within the system where small interventions can lead to big changes. Small interventions can be action points as simple as practicing gratitude, which can then lead to a more powerful change.

While the "Systems Approach" is holistic and comprehensive, there is also "Tall Poppy Syndrome", also known as "Crab mentality", which refers to those individuals within a group who attempt to undermine or sabotage the success of others. When there is a mindset that propagates lack of resources or opportunities, some individuals feel an urgent need to be competitive. Their focus shifts completely on self-preservation, where others' success is viewed as a threat to their own position. It is inevitable that crab mentality fosters distrust and a cycle of negativity.

The human body is an extension of nature, and with similar processes, it organises itself into an intricate interconnected system of cells into tissues into organs. The systems thinking of the human body helps it maintain homeostasis despite external and internal perturbations. Organs do not compete or fight with each other for resources. Tissues do not look down upon each other.

For example, when the gallbladder is removed, our body adapts to the situation by delivering bile directly to the small intestine, ensuring continued digestion. When blood vessels become narrow or there is a blockage, other vessels develop or enlarge to maintain blood flow to the heart muscle.

Just like cells within the human body, human societies are also interconnected and dependent on each other. Actions taken by one country can have ripple effects on other countries. While organs within the body perform specialised functions that contribute to overall health, every country is responsible for contributing to the global economy.

In a similar vein, acts of terrorism, uncontrolled aggression, wars, conflicts, violence, and widespread ecological destruction can be interpreted as the spread of a disease or cancer in the body.

One could also look at "Maslow's Hierarchy of Needs," a systematic model that explores human behaviour through various degrees of motivation. The physiological needs at the foundation of the pyramid enumerate the physical desires of food, clothes, a house, and security, as well as safety needs like financial security. The need for belonging and love is the foundation behind the desire for stable relationships. These desires eventually move to feed how the human feels about himself, and wants others to see him through the needs of self-esteem. Ultimately, moving up the ladder is the pinnacle of desire - self-actualisation.

The stages in the pyramid are not sacrosanct in hierarchy. Each stage can co-exist with another. People keep moving up and down the stages as each need is met. Maslow's hierarchy of needs, when juxtaposed with the stages of evolution in theosophy, presents similar theories.

Kaleidoscope of Kingdoms

According to theosophy, human evolution has taken place over millions of years, travelling from mineral to plant to animal and then to the human kingdom. In essence, evolution is the development of consciousness at different levels. The development is from within, and the catalyst is the circumstance or external environment. Evidently, if there is no internal motivation, there is no growth!

This can be further observed through Arthur E. Powell and his idea of evolution. The theosophical writer, in his book "The Solar System," talks about various types of kingdoms. The senses develop with each kingdom as the consciousness evolves. The mineral kingdom has to endure pain, pressure, cold, heat and other environmental changes, with Powell stating that "In the mineral kingdom, consciousness is a mere 'sub-conscious reaction.' At this level, desire expresses itself as chemical affinity."

The mineral kingdom works on responding to external stimuli, and that is added to the consciousness through resilience, handling pressure, adapting to changes in nature, and developing sensory perception. The attributes of endurance, patience, resilience, and the body's sensory perception are derived through perseverance in the mineral kingdom. In other words, the mineral kingdom functions at a simple, subconscious level, where basic instincts appear as chemical forces. This constant interaction with the physical world helps form the foundation for developing consciousness.

As consciousness evolves into the plant kingdom, there is a development of sensory mechanisms. Photosynthesis is one of the examples of this complex alchemy. Plants provide food, beauty, colours, fragrances, and nutrition to the environment. From roots, they turn into fruits, multiplying within the species. This is what the plant kingdom has added to consciousness! A lot of character traits of the human kingdom have been derived from here. The act of service to oneself and others, community living, beauty in every life form, nurturing, and much more, as learning comes from the plant consciousness.

One must accept that there are principles in nature which impact all life. These hidden rules govern aspects of reality that are not readily apparent or fully explored by humans. Much of life is rooted in the sciences- biology, chemistry, and physics. The law of cause and effect is one such example. Our actions- both big and small- ripple out, setting off a chain reaction of consequences. Whether we realise it, believe it, or ignore it, every choice we make, thought we create, word we speak, has a corresponding effect. This law of karma is based on the principle that every thought, word, and action- good or bad- shapes our future experiences, conditions, and behaviour. What is sown is reaped. This law is exact!

If we pay close attention to the principle of self-sustainability, balance, and regeneration, we understand that nothing goes to waste! Each element plays its part to give and take at different times to maintain the equilibrium. Humans are an extension of this vast ecosystem, intricately connected to each other. We also have the capacity to sustain ourselves-physically, emotionally, socially, mentally, and spiritually.

The reverence and gratitude for this vast interconnectedness were understood by our ancestors too. They never separated themselves from nature, considering themselves as part of the larger cosmos governed by elements. Praying to the deities representing each element was their way of showing gratitude for the role they played in sustaining life. For example, earth was associated with abundance, water with renewal and purification, fire with purification, sacrifice and transformation and air with intellect and communication, ether with intuition. Their blessings were sought for protection and guidance.

> *"All things in nature work silently. They come into being and possess nothing. They fulfil their functions and make no claim."*
>
> **– Lao Tzu**

Modern research agrees that practising gratitude cultivates the same low-self-focus humility Lao Tzu talks about in the above quote. Writing gratitude letters reduces egoic self-attention and measurably boosts humility, and it deepens our felt connection with the natural world, increasing awe, respect, and pro-environmental behaviour.

Simply put, we can tap into the interconnected world and awaken the innate ability to thrive in harmony with ourselves and the world around us. This is when we align ourselves with the ancient wisdom of nature, which is already programmed in the limbic system. The limbic system is that part of the brain which has the ancient, primal consciousness of the animal kingdom packed into it. Being the control centre of all things primal and instinctive, this region is responsible for survival instincts.

When we talk about consciousness, we often think of this uniquely human trait. But here's where it gets interesting, the limbic system is a kind of bridge between the human and all other consciousness. All lower emotions of fear, pride, anger, jealousy, etc are deeply rooted in the evolutionary past.

If one observes, animals have developed various characteristics and behaviours to ensure their survival and reproductive success to continue the race. They have traits to assert themselves, establishing dominance within the social group, displaying prowess, defending territory, and so on.

Circling back to "Maslow's Hierarchy of Needs," it becomes clear that, as animals evolved into humans, the innate drive to assert, gain recognition and achieve success remains the same for both species. He exemplifies the same in his book, 'A Theory of Human Motivation', stating that "All people in our society (with a few pathological exceptions), have a need or desire for a stable, firmly based, usually high evaluation of themselves, for self-respect, or self-esteem, and for the esteem of others."

The desire to display strength, skill, or beauty to attract mates and establish a position in the social hierarchy is no different in chimpanzees and humans. But, while other kingdoms may exhibit behaviours that fulfil lower-level needs of physiological, safety, belonging and esteem needs, at the end of the day, the practice of self-actualisation is uniquely human. Yet, humans are still stuck at the lower realms of the needs ladder.

Arrogance, greed, and pride have led this kingdom to believe it is separate from the rest. Selfish motives and disregard for nature can lead to disharmony and imbalance. Lack of gratitude leads to a sense of entitlement towards the environment around. Recent history is proof that this neglect of interconnectedness has led to disease outbreaks and pandemics.

And then nature has its own way to make humanity learn its lessons. The global pandemic was an opportunity to feel grateful for things we had taken for granted- health, wealth, relationships and so on. It is no brainer that the absence of this reverence or taking the natural resources for granted has led to other crises around the world. Water shortage is one of the examples, considering that seventy per cent of the earth's surface is made up of water. A false sense of entitlement towards resources which are freely available leads to abrasive behaviour of misuse. What we misuse or abuse diminishes. The gifts we hoard for ourselves and do not give away generously are taken away simply because such things are granted to be used for a larger, selfless purpose.

Let us talk facts! Over the past five years, overwhelming evidence shows that, when selfish interests override nature, the environment responds in kind. In the Himalayas and other forested watersheds, deforestation and hasty building driven by "human greed" have amplified lethal flash-floods and landslides. Globally, a UN-backed review found that relentless land clearing and groundwater over-use are turning whole regions into drought "hotspots," compounding hunger and blackouts, while over-extraction and leaky urban systems are driving water shortages and food-price spikes. One should also not forget that COVID-19 traces back to the wildlife trade, where genomic work indicated the virus rode thousands of kilometres via trafficked animals before spilling into humans.

At the centre of this superiority complex is entitlement. Entitlement is a feeling that stems from the belief that one deserves certain privileges without much effort towards the benefits. The root of this feeling lies in social structures and upbringing, apart from various other cultural factors. All of this could stem from "anthropocentrism," which means 'Human-centred,' a view which believes that since humans possess cognitive abilities, they are separate and superior to other kingdoms. Superiority weaves into cultures that emphasise material wealth, individualism, personal success, comparison, and lack of gratitude. The feeling of entitlement also stems from deeper insecurities and unmet emotional needs. Adopting an entitled attitude to assert control or boost self- confidence could have a deeper history of being made to feel powerless or inadequate in the early years.

All is not lost when it comes to our destructive superiority over Mother Nature. Many souls are trying to do their bit to preserve and heal our relationship with it. In Mumbai, India, lawyer Afroz Shah's record-breaking Versova Beach cleanup removed more than 13 million kg of plastic, letting Olive Ridley Sea turtles nest there again after two decades. Aurangabad witnessed an array of incredible women transform the garbage-choked Kham River at Chattrapati Sambhajinagar into 54 acres of lush riparian eco-parks.

The Kauravas Within Us

Ancient texts say, "Some things are increased by being diminished; others are diminished by being increased."

As the great war of the Mahabharat was to begin, both groups of cousins, the Kauravas and the Pandavas, needed to build their own army. For strategic alliances, they were meeting powerful kings to help them in the war. As Duryodhana was gathering his army, he approached Krishna. When he reached Dwarka, the lord was sleeping. Duryodhana, the embodiment of pride and arrogance, sat next to Krishna's head, falsely believing he was not a king, hence not that important. On the other hand, Arjuna, a devotee of Krishna, walks in the room, sees him sleeping, sits next to his feet out of reverence and devotion.

On waking up, Krishna first sees Arjuna and asks for his reason for visiting. Duryodhana makes his presence felt too, but Krishna makes it clear that he will not fight the war. However, he proposed sharing his army of 10000 men among one, and his guidance and support to another. He asked Arjuna to pick whatever he wanted, to which Duryodhana revolted, saying he came first. Krishna reasoned that he had seen Arjuna first, so he deserved the first choice.

After losing an opportunity due to pride and arrogance, Duryodhana was filled with anger. He also feared that Arjuna might take the mighty army. However, Arjuna was full of gratitude towards his beloved teacher. All he wanted was his guru's support, and hence asked only for Krishna's guidance. This made Duryodhana extremely joyous as he won the brawn power of 10000 men.

If there's one thing to learn from this tale, it is that arrogance and pride have a deafening energy. It clouds our sane perspective and is the key ingredient in making people delusional. Have you ever met a person who has poor decision-making skills and is usually lost? It is a delusion that distorts their perception of reality! Delusion brings us to a point where decision-making becomes difficult, and we start making poor choices, believing false information. Poor choices lead to poor interpretation, and poor interpretation leads to poor decisions, something that Duryodhana was guilty of.

Delusion can enable us to perceive others in a distorted way, misread situations, make untrue judgments and so on, resulting in misunderstandings, conflicts, and strained relationships. Over a period, a delusional mind can lead to isolation, alienation and loneliness since others may find it difficult to relate to this distorted version of the person.

Simply speaking, arrogance, excessive pride, and lack of humility are like the dirt on the windscreen, impairing your ability to navigate life and function effectively. It is a path of slow self-destruction. Over time, these destructive tendencies can prevent us from fulfilling our deeper psychological needs. This is where theories like Maslow's help us chart the path from basic survival towards higher levels of personal growth.

Maslow's theory stacks the lower needs from a deprivation point of view; hence, a person will not move up till the basic needs are met. When the basic needs are satiated, there is a desire for growth. The distinctive characteristic of human consciousness to transcend the lower desires is self-actualisation. It is nothing like any other kingdom.

While Maslow describes self-actualisation as the highest level of fulfilment, there are schools of thought which take this idea further. According to J Krishnamurti, physical evolution has reached its end, and humans can only grow on a psychological level now. He further elaborated that we need a revolution of the psyche and do not need to wait for millions of years for evolution.

The revolution of the human psyche lies in rising above lower needs and moving beyond mere survival instincts. We are forever entangled in the loop of survival-safety-esteem. This perpetual repeat mode is not letting humans realise their own immense potential. As the Bible states, "Man shall not live by bread alone". Bread is just the means to satisfy and help the physical body function achieve the goals of the mind.

Self -actualisation as a path is also known as self-realisation. This ought to be the aim of human beings- knowing who we really are and understanding the ability to get there. Think about this! We work to make our body comfortable by satisfying their needs. However, what is the use of that body when it ultimately dies?

This is why most cultures impress upon the idea that our body is just a vehicle of the soul. We are willing passengers on this vehicle, and yet we never get curious to know who is driving the vehicle! The desire to take that journey of self-discovery and stay put on the path is self-actualisation. It takes many incarnations to get to know ourselves, work on ourselves, and become a perfected being. This work is meant to disentangle one from the grips of the lower consciousness, which leads to identification with the body's needs, fears, limitations, and weaknesses. The most important task of the human kingdom is to purify this vehicle in terms of physical, emotional, and mental negative impressions as well as limitations.

Limitations are the true enemies of the self! We have 100 Kauravas within us. Anger, jealousy, guilt, fear, arrogance, violence, laziness, procrastination, pride, resentment, depression, loneliness, hatred, sadness, to name a few. Alternatively, the Pandavas within us represent the 5 senses. The body's senses must diminish the urges of the lower tendencies with the help of the higher consciousness of the soul, as represented by Krishna.

According to Paramhamsa Yogananda, "Self-realisation is knowing in all parts of the body, mind and soul that you have the kingdom of God that you do not have to pray that it comes to you; that God's omnipresence is your omnipresence; and that all that you need to do is improve your knowing"

This means there is a larger aspect to one's physical body, feelings, and thoughts. Humans need to recognise this powerful aspect, whether we call it God, the higher self, soul, or energy, and realize that the human body exists within this energy.

Considering the above, one can infer that omnipresence is the basis of interconnectedness. Whatever you want in life, you do not have to pray for it to come to you. You achieve what you desire when you become it! When you make that desire an inherent part of your being and do not think of it as something separate or outside of you, it is like experiencing the presence of God's power within you. To build this, one needs to work on expanding the power of awareness.

Authenticity Over Approval

You cannot know anything without knowing yourself. This idea is the root of all philosophical and spiritual teachings. Ancient Greek philosophers famously emphasised the importance of self-awareness and self-knowledge. The Delphic maxim "Know thyself" (γνῶθι σαυτόν) is inscribed on the Temple of Apollo at Delphi, Greece, serving as the foundation of Greek philosophical thought. Philosopher Socrates famously adopted this perception to his philosophical mission, arguing that the unexamined life is not worth living. "Knowing yourself" enables us to make successful choices, live authentically, true to one's nature, and to find the purpose of one's existence.

It is an undeniable truth that inauthentic living involves self-deception. Deceiving oneself to conform to the standards of the immediate social environment, community, or family, is a common norm. This program is in place to lock the individuals within the boundaries of social acceptance, status, or approval, making it easier to control members of the group. The larger motive could also be to work towards perfection or success as a norm idealised by the whole group. However, in the process of conforming, one starts to live an inauthentic life, striving for an empty idea of success by ignoring imperfections, vulnerabilities, fear of failure or inadequacy.

Young people are more vulnerable to the pressures of self-deception in today's day and age.

Rohan, a typical Indian teenager, always wore a frown and kept grumbling through his days. He compared himself to classmates with new phones, branded shoes, or more pocket money. His parents' constant "no" made him irritable and indignant.

One evening, at a friend's house, he noticed the father coming home late, exhausted. His friend rushed to hug him. He whispered, "I am grateful to my father. He works hard, late at night too, so we can get a better life." That night, Rohan looked at his parents differently. Instead of what they did not give, he saw what they sacrificed. He started concentrating on his studies and appreciating everything he was given.

The by-product of not living an authentic life is pretence, self-inflation, and a complete lack of self-awareness, which results in incongruence. When one acts opposite to one's beliefs and values, and constantly justifies it.

Research shows that inauthenticity is a strong predictor of aggressive behaviour. In conflict situations, authentic individuals are likely to choose conflict-solving strategies that consider their own and others' needs. They are less likely to be negatively affected by conflicts. Further, as their ego-involvement is lower, authentic individuals are less likely to engage in verbal defensiveness, show less destructive reactions to hypothetical partner transgressions, and respond less aggressively in unfair situations. Their constructive approach to feedback provides a source of self-esteem to social partners, who feel that their thoughts and suggestions are taken seriously.

In the "Handbook of Positive Psychology", Snyder and Lopez also summarise that authenticity can also be described as approving one's true self, and representing that exact image, value, belief, and behaviour to oneself and others. It is about representing self sincerely, speaking the facts but more precisely genuinely presenting yourself, behaving honestly. It is about taking responsibility for your emotions and actions.

We must also understand the contrast between the concept of authentic living and the effect of external influences. Authentic-living involves being true to oneself most of the time and behaving in most situations that are consistent with one's own values and beliefs. Whereas, accepting external influences describes the beliefs that a person must adjust to the expectations of others. Authentic-living is a sign of a feeling of authenticity; in contrary, self-alienation by accepting external influences shows inauthenticity (Pinto et al., 2012; Wood et al., 2008). Wood et al. (2008) found that authenticity has a positive correlation with subjective well-being, psychological well-being, and self-esteem and two subscales of the authenticity scale, while accepting external influence and self-alienation were positively correlated with anxiety and stress.

Compared to those who live a self-alienated life, authentic individuals report higher levels of self-esteem, positive affect, life satisfaction, interpersonal trust, work engagement, task performance, and organisational citizenship behaviours.

"Whatever happens in your life, no matter how troubling things might seem, do not enter the neighbourhood of despair. Even when all doors remain closed, God will open up a new path only for you. Be thankful! It is easy to be thankful when all is well. A Sufi is thankful not only for what he has been given but also for all that he has been denied."

– Shams E Trabrizi (Persian Sufi and a roaming dervish), 40 Rules of love.

Reflecting upon the above quote, one realises that being grateful for what has been denied is very challenging, and yet an enriching practice. This is where we can test the true value of our gratitude and know if we have imbibed it or not. The practice of gratitude is more transformative during tough periods. Difficult times may not align with our expectations, but reflecting on denied desires can help shift our perspective from what we lack to the blessings and opportunities presented in our lives at that moment.

This positive opportunity is right at the foot of our door. Even if it may not be in the awareness or the consciousness, this gift is presented for the attitude of acceptance and adaptability. Confronting denial with bravery can spark self-discovery and personal growth. Challenges often reveal our preparation, the gap between what we believe and how we act eventually. By confronting them, we can gain deeper insight into our capabilities and push our self-belief boundaries.

Dwelling on disappointments is a black hole from which we can spiral down to helplessness and hopelessness. Focusing on what went wrong is a button that, when pressed, opens a Pandora's box of past triggers, while also sapping our energy and beginning to reinforce negative experiences onto us.

During such testing times, there are only two options- either keep the bitterness going and go downhill with physical and psychological health, or surrender to the belief that everything happens for a reason, even if one may not be able to understand it fully at that time.

The Science of Waiting

When you do not get what you want, it could be because of circumstances beyond your immediate awareness or control. The bigger task at hand is how to respond to it. Consciously accepting that the fulfilment will happen, just that it's delayed, leads to building patience, resilience, self-discipline, and long-term goal orientation.

This practice is also known as delayed gratification, an important tool in our mental arsenal. Conscious acceptance of delayed gratification is the ability to ride over immediate desires, rather than giving in to the thirst for instant gratification, which, over a period, leads to frustration and stress.

One of the most famous studies on delayed gratification is the "Stanford Marshmallow Experiment" by psychologist Walter Mischel. In this study, children were offered a choice between receiving one marshmallow immediately or waiting for a short period (15minutes) to receive two marshmallows. The researchers found that children who were able to hold for a little longer, delay gratification and wait for the larger reward tended to have better outcomes in terms of academic achievement, health, and social success later in life.

Delayed gratification helps in building cognitive skills and impulse control. Neuroscientific research backs these insights. Brain imaging studies have shown that regions of the prefrontal cortex are activated when individuals engage in tasks requiring delayed gratification. The prefrontal cortex is a critical part of the brain involved in various complex cognitive functions and behaviours such as executive functions of planning, problem-solving and goal-directed behaviours as well as impulse control, attention, and focus. Working memory functions of reasoning, comprehension, and learning. Social behaviour tools such as interpreting social cues, empathy and maintaining social relationships. Emotional regulation functions like maintaining emotional stability and managing emotional responses, as well as decision making, moral and ethical reasoning and future planning. The pre-frontal cortex is critical for all cognitive functions essential for daily life, it is crucial in enabling humans to think, plan, adapt and socialise.

Being grateful for something which you think has been denied shifts the perspective to the true path and not the one you assumed to be the only one. You have a goal, and there are many paths leading in that direction. Which path you take is charted by an individual's free will. You need to be aware that there are many choices available to us, and the one we choose determines the time and effort we take to get to the goal.

Not getting something you were hoping for is a clear sign that either the time is not right, or there is not enough effort, or the path is not right. There is something better and bigger to be learned or achieved. Hence, develop patience and perseverance. Wait for the bigger picture to unfold. In the meantime, be grateful for what you did not get, because that would not only have shortchanged you, but also wasted your time and effort. The most common place where this can be applied is our professional life.

Riya, a mid-level executive, felt stuck in her current job. "Nothing works out for me", is what she always thought. She scrolled through social media, envying friends who seemed luckier, richer, happier.

Her happier older cousin listened to her struggle and suggested, "When you feel stuck, do not push harder. Pause and notice what is already working for you. Start by writing three things you are grateful for daily, however small, and three things you want. Write them with gratitude as if you already have them". Weeks later, opportunities started opening — an interview, new friendships, and appreciation from colleagues.

Riya realised gratitude was an energy amplifier. What she appreciated expanded, almost as if the universe was responding: "If you value it, I'll give you more."

The core of patience and perseverance is to trust that great things are eventually in store. We just need to have faith and, more importantly, a meaning and purpose.

"Man's search for meaning" is a book written by Viktor E. Frankl, a psychiatrist and Holocaust survivor. This book has had a profound impact on readers around the world for its insights into resilience and man's quest for meaning. Frankl detailed certain insights and principles to apply in life:

- Finding Meaning and Purpose-
  - He emphasised that finding meaning even in suffering, and having a clear purpose in life, can help people endure the most difficult situations.
- Choosing the right attitude-
  - Even in the direst of circumstances, individuals have the freedom to choose their attitude and their response to the situation.
- Engaging in meaningful activities-
  - To enrich one's life with a sense of purpose and fulfilment, one must consciously engage in meaningful activities other than mundane work
- Self-Transcendence-
  - Shift the focus beyond your own concerns to something greater than yourself.

Finding meaning in every act is the ultimate form of conscious living. The act may be as incidental as thinking, speaking, behaving, engaging, or working. Further to this, one must also assign a purpose to every small act and to life itself. Living without purpose is the most detrimental and demeaning thing we as humans can do. Even animals live with a purpose, and so do plants.

Once an individual uncovers the meaning behind every small act and discovers their true purpose, there will be no room for unfulfilled expectations, disappointment, or helplessness. Purpose, along with a positive mindset and attitude, can significantly impact one's ability to unfold their destiny. Maintaining optimism, a growth-oriented mindset, and gratitude for everything can help individuals overcome any obstacle and achieve their goals.

By integrating gratitude and humility in life, one transcends self-centred concerns and connects with a larger purpose. One has no control over their immediate environment, as there are many other variables involved. Spending time and effort on fears, doubts and worries does not change the situation; in fact, it makes our thoughts far more morbid and worse. Instead, focusing on a higher purpose fosters resilience and helps build momentum towards a positive outlook. With this attitude, the problem ceases to exist.

Gratitude is more than a fleeting emotion, an exercise, or an occasional practice. It is a profound state of being that can transform how you perceive and interact with the world. You may perceive something different and act differently according to the situation or person; however, if you are not feeling gratitude from within, the lack of authenticity will show up. When gratitude becomes ingrained in our being, it influences how we approach everything and everyone in life daily.

Wired For Wonder

Imagine this! An early human hunter-gatherer, belonging to the times when tribes relied on hunting and foraging for survival. While foraging for berries near a forest, he hears rustling in the bushes. Suddenly, a large, aggressive tiger emerges from the foliage, staring directly at him. What happens next? This is the trigger for the fight or flight response inside all humans:

- The sight and sound of the tiger trigger his brain's amygdala, the region involved in processing emotions.
- The amygdala assesses the threat and sends a distress signal to the hypothalamus, the brain's command system for autonomic functions.
- The hypothalamus activates the sympathetic nervous system by sending signals from the autonomic nerves to the adrenal glands, located above the kidneys.
- Adrenals release hormones such as adrenaline and noradrenaline into the bloodstream.

This exhilarating encounter also results in various physiological changes in the body:

1. Cardiovascular system:
    - The adrenaline release increases the heart rate and blood pressure, because the heart is contracting faster to ensure

more blood (oxygen and nutrition) is delivered to the vital organs
- Blood vessels to non-essential systems such as the digestive tract constrict, while those supporting the muscles dilate, optimising blood flow where it is most needed.

2. Respiratory system:
   - Rate and depth of the breathing increases known as hyperventilation. This supplies more oxygen to the blood and expels carbon dioxide more quickly, preparing the body for increased physical exercise

3. Muscular system:
   - Muscles throughout the body tense up, primed for action. This can lead to feelings of tightness or tension.

4. Metabolic changes:
   - Cortisol, known as the "stress hormone", is released by the adrenal glands. It increases glucose in the bloodstream. Glycogen stores in the liver are broken down into glucose, providing a quick source of energy. Fat stores are mobilised, releasing fatty acids into the bloodstream for fuel.
   - Overall metabolic rate of the body increases, ensuring that the body has enough energy to sustain physical exertion

5. Digestive system:
   - Digestion slows or stops, as the blood flow is redirected from the gastrointestinal tract to the muscles and brain. This can result in dry mouth and reduced digestive activity.

6. Sensory Enhancement:
    - Pupils dilate to more light into the eyes, hearing and other senses become more acute, making the individual more aware of the environment.
7. Cognitive Effect:
    - Cognitive focus shifts to immediate threat, potentially impairing the ability to think long-term or perform complex tasks
8. Emotional Response:
    - Fear, anxiety or aggression may be experienced depending on the coping mechanism of the individual.
9. Equilibrium:
    - Once the threat is perceived to be gone, the parasympathetic nervous system kicks in to calm the body and return to a state of homeostasis or equilibrium.
    - This promotes the 'Rest and Digest' response, slowing the heart rate, reducing the blood pressure, and restoring the digestion and immune system.

Coming back to the early human hunter, he has two options: to fight the tiger or flee. Both options stem from a survival mindset. Today, we face fewer physical threats; however, the fight or flight response still gets activated due to daily stressors such as work deadlines, relationship conflicts, and financial pressure, as this response is deeply rooted in our brain's limbic system, referred to as the primitive brain.

In today's times, humans don't physically fight or flee for survival, hence it has psychological effects. The hormones released during stressful episodes are not fully utilised, leading to many psycho-somatic diseases, which lead to:

- **Cardiovascular Strain**- Persistent high levels of adrenaline increase heart rate and blood pressure, thereby increasing the risk of hypertension, heart diseases, and stroke.
- **Immune System Suppression**- Chronic stress suppresses the immune system, making the body susceptible to illnesses and infection.
- **Metabolic Imbalance**- Increased cortisol levels influence metabolism by increasing blood sugar levels. Over time, this leads to insulin resistance, weight gain, and type 2 diabetes
- **Muscle Pain and Tension**- As the energy is sent to the muscles when the sympathetic nervous system is triggered, the rising stress over time leads to constant muscle tension without release, causing headaches, back pain, and general muscle stiffness.
- **Mental health issues**- High levels of stress hormones are associated with anxiety, depression, and other mood disorders. The overactivation of the brain and senses can lead to impaired cognitive functions.
- **Digestive problems**- Since the digestive system is slowed down, prolonged, unchecked stress can lead to acidity, irritable bowel movement, reflux and other gastrointestinal diseases.

Understanding the body and mind's response to fight or flight situations and knowing its long-term effects can help individuals recognise the signs of stress and take proactive steps to course correct. Some of the key things that can address stress are:

- Introducing discipline in lifestyle by following eight hours of sleep, a regular exercise schedule, and a balanced diet.
- Regulating the brain, hormones, and emotions by practising awareness in the moment.
- Identifying triggers leading to unpleasant situations and applying mindfulness in every activity.
- Abdominal breathing exercises, meditation and journaling have also proved to develop coping mechanisms.

Research shows that practising gratitude can lead to improved life and mental health, while lending us a better understanding of the reasons for stress, enhanced emotional regulation, a positive mindset and much more. All one needs to do is tap into the immense, understated power of gratitude.

The idea of gratitude as a superpower leading to the realisation of our goals may sound a bit far-fetched or mystical, but there is solid scientific backing to it. When we express gratitude, our brains release dopamine and serotonin. These are neurotransmitters and hormones associated with happiness. Feelings and expression of gratitude can regulate cortisol, which is a stress hormone. Expressing gratitude is an antidote to depression.

Gratitude can draw us silver linings from the bleakest of situations.

Neha was exhausted from dealing with her husband's drinking. Between handling the kids, her job, and the late-night chaos, she felt hate, stuck, and resentful.

One evening, while venting to a close friend, the friend said gently, "I know it's hard. Even in this storm, is there one thing you can still be grateful for? Do you see light somewhere? And remember, you always have many choices. That night, instead of replaying the anger and the blame, Neha remembered how her husband is a caring father during sober days and how he is struggling himself to find a way out.

She looked at him asleep and whispered, "Thank you for the peaceful moments and just being around the children. I pray that you find your way back."

She stopped the internal struggle and gave hope a choice. Her children no longer saw a bitter, burdened mother- they saw someone calmer, more centred. Being grateful for what she had cleared her mind, helping her respond instead of react. She made better choices for herself and her kids. Instead of blaming the situation, she began reclaiming her old self.

Gratitude has an immediate impact and long-lasting shift in various aspects of life, including stress management, emotions, physical health, mental well-being, social connections, relationships, and even financial matters. In essence, what gratitude does is:

1. **Shifts focus**:
    - Regular practice of gratitude shifts perspective from what's not working or negative emotions to positive emotions such as joy, contentment, and happiness.

- By focusing on things one is grateful for, individuals shift their perspective from scarcity to abundance, dislike to likes, hatred to love, sadness to joy and so forth.

2. **Improves physical health**:
   - Research suggests that practising gratitude over time can improve physical health by reducing symptoms of illnesses, lowering blood pressure, and boosting the immune system.
   - Focusing on positive emotions reduces stress, hence enhancing immunity.

3. **Detoxifies our body**:
   - Regular practice of gratitude reduces cortisol levels in the body, reducing the physical and psychological effects of stress.
   - This practice activates the parasympathetic nervous system, which helps the body to relax and recover from stress

4. **Improves sleep**:
   - Being in a state of gratitude and consciously practising the discipline of expressing gratitude before bedtime can reduce the overload on the conscious mind.
   - Individuals may experience reduced anxiety and rumination, leading to sound sleep.

5. **Reduces risk of depression and anxiety**:
   - Gratitude interventions have shown to be effective in reducing symptoms of depression and anxiety. Regularly acknowledging and appreciating the good things in life can

help magnify the positive aspects and counteract negative thought patterns, promoting emotional resilience.

6. **Enhances neurobiological health**:
   - What makes Gratitude a superpower is that the practice deeply focuses on mindfulness, awareness, and presence in the moment, which is the secret behind ancient yogic practices. This is the foundation of Dharna and Dhyaan, or loosely put, awareness and concentration.
   - Gratitude practices have been found to increase activity in the brain regions associated with reward, such as the medial prefrontal cortex.

7. **Strengthens relationships**:
   - Some people are better at keeping healthy relationships, and the key to this is appreciating others and giving credit. When individuals receive recognition for their contributions, it significantly boosts morale and motivation.
   - A study published in the Journal of Personality and Social Psychology found that gratitude is a powerful predictor of relationship satisfaction.
   - When loved ones feel appreciated, they are more likely to communicate openly and positively.

8. **Creates a safe space for oneself and others**:
   - Trust is fundamental for any interaction, healthy relationship, or work. A sense of security is developed when one expresses gratitude for each other's efforts and contributions.

9. **Elevates work satisfaction**:
   - A meta-analysis by Harari, Reaves, and Viswesvaran (2016) showed that job satisfaction is significantly related to job performance. When employees feel valued, their job satisfaction increases, leading to better performance and lower turnover rates.
   - A study published in the Journal of Applied Psychology found that gratitude and recognition in the workplace lead to higher levels of cooperation and altruistic behaviour among team members.

10. **Brings clarity and focus**:
    - The formula of success is clarity and focus on a few things and deleting what does not serve anyone. Counting blessings, being thankful for achievements, individuals develop a bird's eye view on their priorities, strengths and vision. This allows a better strategy and pouring energies into relevant tasks more effectively.

11. **Gives motivation**:
    - A goal cannot be achieved without motivation. Motivation can come from extrinsic factors or intrinsic passion.
    - Gratitude serves as a powerful motivator by reinforcing confidence in abilities and validation of good.
    - Perseverance and determination to continue with the effort come from acknowledging how one has reached so far.

Gratitude is a mindset, a virtue, and a habit. It is not a superficial practice suggested by a popular life coach or a new fad. It is also not a flaky thank-you note. It is about shifting awareness to things which are positive and in the flow. It is about being aware, recognising and feeling good towards people, things, events, circumstances and appreciating everything in life, whether big or insignificant, tangible, or intangible, entitled or achieved.

You Can Move Mountains!

There are a flock of practical and effective methods to integrate gratitude into daily life and enhance mental clarity, emotional stability, growth mindset and proactive behaviour. These small and digestible approaches rewire the brain to navigate life more efficiently, leading individuals to their highest potential.

Gratitude indeed is a superpower, and, when nurtured, it has an immense potential to bring out a higher version of oneself. How can one practice gratitude regularly in the smallest of ways? The answer's quite simple:

Gratitude Journaling

Journaling connects the mind to the body. We engage in semantic encoding when we write, as we crystalize the thoughts by attaching meaning and feelings through words. This process activates various parts of the brain. The power of the thought is carried through the written words. Writing physically manifests thoughts, intentions, and feelings.

- What's the best way to turn gratitude journaling into a daily habit? Make it a bedtime ritual!

- Keep a journal at your bedside. An ideal time to make the entries is before sleeping when the mind is relaxed, and whatever you will journal will go down in the subconscious mind. This will program the mind with positive suggestions.
- Start by getting into a positive and calm frame of mind. Focus on emotions of joy, contentment, happiness, love, etc. Gratitude is a feeling, and when that is identified and poured into the writing, it becomes magical.
- You can write about anything you are grateful for, being specific always goes deeper in the psyche. Look at various aspects of life. You can start with that particular day or life in general.
- Journal your personal growth and achievements, like specific accomplishments (e.g., completing a challenging project, mastering a new skill), personal qualities you are proud of (e.g., resilience, creativity) and lessons learned from difficult situations.
  - "Today, I'm grateful for completing my first 5K run. It showed me how much my endurance has improved."
  - "I'm thankful for learning to stay calm under pressure during today's meeting."

- Our relationships play a key role in making us who we are. Write about the relationships that are an intrinsic part of your life.
  - State the acts of kindness received from friends or family (e.g., a supportive conversation, a thoughtful gesture).
  - Speak about shared experiences (e.g., a memorable outing, a deep conversation).

  - Jot down the qualities you appreciate in others (e.g., a friend's sense of humour, a partner's patience).
    - "I'm grateful for my friend Sarah, who listened to me vent today and created a safe space."
    - "I appreciate my partner for the coffee this morning."
- A healthy mind and body is a gift that should be cherished. Never forget to journal about health and well-being.
  - Journal about the positive changes in your health (e.g., feeling more energetic, recovering from an illness).
  - Talk about enjoyable physical activities (e.g., a refreshing walk, a great workout), and mental health milestones (e.g., managing stress, experiencing a sense of calm).
    - "I appreciate myself for not letting the external chaos affect my mood"
    - "I appreciate my body's ability to go a bit further in today's exercise routine."
- It's always helpful to note down our daily comforts and pleasures. The little things that bring us glee and satisfaction.
  - Simple joys (e.g., a delicious meal, a comfortable bed).
  - Moments of beauty (e.g., a stunning sunset, a beautiful piece of music).
  - Small victories (e.g., finding a good parking spot, having a productive day).
    - "I'm grateful for the warm meal my helper served me while I could finish the other chores"
    - "I am thankful for the crisp air, bright sunshine and that I could finish my work earlier to experience this joy"

- Journal your opportunities and experiences! Nothing beats a recollection of things to look forward to, and things you've loved to do.
    - Growth opportunities (e.g., a new job opportunity, a chance to travel).
    - New experiences (e.g., trying a new hobby, meeting new people).
    - Educational opportunities (e.g., attending a workshop, learning something new).
        - "I'm thankful to my boss for the opportunity to attend a fascinating seminar on mindfulness today."
        - "I'm grateful to my best buddy for taking me to a new hiking trail and putting up with my pace"
- Planet Earth is the only home we have. To express our love for nature and surroundings is always a good idea.
    - Nature's beauty (e.g., a clear blue sky, blooming flowers).
    - Positive aspects of your living environment (e.g., a cosy home, a friendly neighbourhood).
    - Environmental factors (e.g., good weather, clean air).
        - "I appreciate the vibrant colours of the autumn leaves on my walk today."
        - "I'm grateful to the house I live in. I acknowledge every room, walls and furniture"

Expressing gratitude for goals "not yet" achieved

The practice of being grateful for things yet not achieved is the secret to speeding up manifestation. It cultivates a goal-oriented mindset and is in a zone of goal already achieved. The faith and positivity it offers to the process fuel the thoughts and actions towards the direction. All one needs to do is:

- Everything begins with a thought! Create a thought of your goal; how would it look when achieved, what will you feel?
  - Sit in a comfortable, quiet place, imagine a TV screen in front of your closed eyes. This TV is projecting a movie where you are the hero, and you have just achieved your goal.
  - Picture every detail -the moment, outcome and emotion. Spice the thoughts with emotions of achievement, joy, gratitude, and excitement. Feel it in every bone
  - Physicalise this by expressing your gratitude on paper in the present tense with emotions.
    - "I am so grateful to my boss for the promotion and the increment at work. I am happy, and I bless my boss"
  - You could also create a vision board for the goal with images and words that represent your goal.
  - Spend a few minutes every day being thankful for the manifestation of the same.
  - Celebrate small wins towards the larger goal. Do not let doubt, self-sabotaging thinking and fear ruin this exercise. Be patient and believe it has happened.
  - Align your thoughts, behaviour, emotions, and actions with the goal.

Gratitude time with family

Another way to develop gratitude is by making a ritual out of the practice with family members. It's not in the daily hustle that we remember to appreciate our family for small selfless acts they do out of love, concern, and care. Especially parents.

Here's a way to acknowledge the same when they are around us:

- All family members sit in a way that everyone can see each other
- Individuals write on a sheet of paper: "I am grateful to ... Because you..."
    - "I am grateful to dad because you always listen to me without judgment and encourage me to think"
    - "I am grateful to you, my son, for keeping your room tidy. That gives me time relief and time to finish other chores"
- Encourage members to write details, give examples and express feelings
- Once the writing is done, each family member reads the message aloud, looking into the eyes of the person it has been written for.
- This exercise creates a safe space to say things which go unnoticed or unsaid.

Gratitude exercise with the partner

The most important link to harmony in a relationship is communication. Gratitude exercise is a way to acknowledge your partner and all those small yet significant things that go unnoticed, unappreciated, and then blow up, leading to being unheard.

- Here is what partners can do:
  - Make time for Gratitude practice before dinner
  - Look into the eyes of your partner
  - Feel the gratitude within
  - Verbalise your thoughts: "I am grateful to you for/because..."
- What we give is what comes back, so it's intelligent to say what you want to come back to you.

Gratitude letters to your work team

Not being acknowledged is the most repetitive reason for employees to quit. Showing gratitude in the workplace does not leave the manager weak or the team members more powerful. It is a genuine human need to be acknowledged and recognised.

- This can be done formally through emails or personalised letters.
- Practice of gratitude towards employees, partners and customers is a way to harvest the fruits of loyalty and trust.

Gratitude Meditation

Take a few moments in the day to pause and reflect on small and big things, moments, people, nature, achievements, etc during mundane, routine activities. Meditation is a state of a higher degree of focus coupled with awareness. Meditating on being grateful for everything is a practice which makes it more organic, brings it alive and makes it part of the being. Anyone can do it! You don't need guided meditation for this. You just need to:

- Sit or lie down in a comfortable and quiet place where you will not be disturbed. Close your eyes and take several deep breaths from the abdomen.
- Centre yourself, focus on your breathing and relax your body. Imagine you are in your own sanctuary: a safe space which belongs to you.
- Engage your senses! Be aware of the touch of the clothes, sounds, and pleasant smell. Allow the emotions of gratitude, joy and happiness to fill your being.
- Remind yourself about all your achievements, people in your life who have supported, helped and expressed love to you. Be aware of the positive feelings and reflect on things you are grateful for.
- With your closed eyes, thank the universe, people, places you have visited, situations presented to you, nature, weather, your body, and whatever you wish to focus on:
  - "I'm grateful to my body for healthy functioning. I am grateful for a good immune system. I thank my eyes for a perfect vision. I thank my heart for beating and pumping blood."
  - "I'm grateful to body parts for good digestion. I am grateful for my blood to be purified. I am grateful for good muscles and bones. I am grateful for a clear and sharp mind. I am grateful for my good memory. I am grateful for each body part to function perfectly."
  - "I'm grateful for the sun, water, earth and air. I'm thankful for the healthy food that energises me. I'm grateful for a well-balanced life."
  - "I'm grateful to have such supportive parents."

- "I'm grateful for the challenging situations in my life. They are bringing out the best in me. Thank you, universe, for giving me a sharp mind, courage and strength to learn my lessons fast."
- "I'm grateful for my partner to help me in my journey, for the kindness and care."
- "I'm thankful for simply waking up every morning with the zest to live my life full and beyond.

How much is too much?

While gratitude is one of the most potent sources of transformation known to mankind, like all things in life, when misused or wrongly applied, it can distort into something less than healthy. Here are a few ways to avoid abusing the immense power that gratitude holds:

Don't force it!

There are instances when, despite harbouring a lot of pain inside or facing legitimate struggles, people are told to buckle up and be blindly 'grateful'. The idea of gratitude is not dismiss suffering, but to acknowledge and work along with it to solve the issue and heal. In true gratitude, we don't ignore challenges, but identify how to deal with them, while always remembering the silver linings.

Don't misinterpret it!

Gratitude should never be used as a shield to accept toxicity, injustice, or unhealthy environments. Being grateful for life's blessings doesn't mean tolerating abuse or refusing to take action when change is needed. Authentic gratitude empowers rather than imprisons. One must never confuse the true purpose behind gratitude.

Don't fake it!

Gratitude is a positive energy. Exercising it without genuine feeling or using it as a trend can not only dilute its power, but also have a butterfly effect on your life in other ways. Gratitude must come from the heart, from truly noticing, feeling, and acknowledging, it risks becoming performative.

Don't overuse it!

Yes! There is indeed a thing such as "too much gratitude". Just like with other things in life, balance is the gateway to a healthy relationship with gratitude. We must not aimlessly shower our superpower of gratitude without evaluating the need and necessity of the same. Remember, be grateful most of the time, but don't be grateful all the time! Choose balance over abundance.

An effective real-world case study of how blind and excessive gratitude had dire consequences could be examined by the case of WeWork. At WeWork, employees and investors were swept up in Adam Neumann's charismatic vision-and felt deeply grateful just to be part of the company's mission. This loyalty muted critical oversight, allowed erratic, unsustainable decisions, and contributed to a dramatic collapse when the IPO failed, and valuations plummeted.

Writing The Wrongs

Some anecdotes inspire us to take action. Ekta's story could be one such example. Ekta had been feeling overwhelmed by the mounting stress at work, long hours, conflicts within the family and pressure she put on herself to excel in everything.

Priya, her close friend, noticed Ekta's withdrawal from life and gave her a gratitude journal. Though sceptical at first and in complete denial, Ekta promised Priya that she would write 3 things she was grateful for each day.

At first, she struggled to find the positives amid the turmoil, disappointments and a gimmick. She struggled. It felt awkward and forced. However, it was the lowest of the lows, and she wanted to show commitment and determination to herself.

1. I am grateful for the warm breakfast cooked by Mom with love and concern
2. I am thankful to breathe each day in comfort
3. I am so grateful for the funny Instagram reels shared at the office.

As days passed by, Ekta found herself looking forward to her nighttime ritual of being thankful for things, however small. She was noticing things which she previously had taken for granted or was entitled.

With each entry, her perspective began to shift. Her problems didn't disappear magically; they no longer consumed her mentally and emotionally. She realised that while she couldn't control everything that happened to her, she could focus on what was working for her and manage her response.

The gratitude journal became her safe space, which captured the light in the world that seemed dark. It gave her a sense of perspective. She felt happier. This also slowly changed the situation around her as she started attracting better times.

Scaling the peak of pure gratitude may be tough, but once you reach the top and look back, the whole journey will feel like a lesson. A lesson in adopting gratitude as a daily part of our life, a lesson in being grateful during the most challenging moments, and a lesson in focusing on the blessings we have, rather than the things we don't.

After imbuing gratitude into our entire being, the next step we need to take is embrace kindness, embrace empathy, and the whole concept of compassion.

The Second Super Power

COMPASSION

Lead with The Heart

An emotion hardwired in humans since birth is compassion. It helps us relate to other living things, their situations, and encourages us to take action in making situations better for others. But, once the complexities of modern life take over, humans forget this life-changing super power, rather choosing a "survival of the fittest" mindset that unleashes selfishness and competitiveness.

Ironically, while the term 'Survival of the Fittest' is often attached with Charles Darwin, in reality, he wasn't even behind coining the term. Introduced by social philosopher Herbert Spencer, the term was later used by Darwin as a synonym for natural selection, but he never considered it anything more than a short explanatory phrase.

If "survival of the fittest" was the reason for survival, then the definition of fittest from birth is 'Compassion'. The most compassionate will survive without having to try hard. There are some strengths which develop due to certain upbringing, environment and culture, and there are certain superpowers which come as a default setting in our human software. Compassion is one such rare gem that is pre-installed in our system, a gem that needs to be nurtured and cultivated with each experience.

For centuries, we have been conditioned, brainwashed and inundated by the concept of 'Survival of the fittest' as the path to success and evolution. We need to first tread into the truth that "survival of the fittest" isn't actually about the strongest hand defeating others through dominance, but rather, it is simply the ability to reproduce. It is not about any setting of cruelty.

This misunderstood theory is at the root of today's needlessly cutthroat 'Survival' mindset, suggesting that the most competitive, adaptable and strongest individuals stand a chance to make it. A vast majority of today's society is structured on this false idea. The world is serving us quasi-compelling justifications to promote mindless competition, hierarchical structures, pushover growth, hollow confidence, brazen economic growth, and this has led to a world which is broken and divided.

Nowadays, the focus is on competing with others, prioritising short-term gains and a hustle culture. There will always be some justification, for example, there are only "that many jobs", or there is a "huge population" waiting for a small number of vacancies. Basically, all resources are limited, hence we should grab our bit.

This is relevant politically too, as countries are in a constant "survival mode", dependent on military might, economic dominance and other coercions that inevitably lead to global tensions and conflicts. 'Survival of the fittest' has promoted a world where success is defined by one's ability to outcompete others, completely ignoring collective well-being.

To go deeper into this theory, one must first ask what is the definition of 'Fittest'? In the traditional sense, it is the capacity to endure physical challenges and avoid predation. It is also the ability to adapt to changing environments without external resources. It looks at resources as scarce and deeply focuses on competing for food, mates, shelter, and territory. Also, the rare chance of producing offspring that can survive. This is a primitive mode which governs our limbic brain and makes it operate in fight or flight mode. This perception is not newfound either; civilisations after civilisations in the past have also viewed 'fitness' in a similar vein.

Inherently, survival mode is designed to keep an individual looking for immediate gains, the body undergoes a series of physiological changes designed to respond to the dynamic environment. The body and mind are set on the fight (Aggressive) or flight (Avoidant) response, regulated by the sympathetic nervous system. A comprehensive study by the Cleveland Clinic, USA, also supports this idea. The study explicitly concludes that danger or stress activates the "fight or flight" response in us, increasing our heart rate, redirecting blood to skeletal muscles, dilating pupils, and slowing digestion. All involuntary changes to maximise survival potential".

The response to a survival scenario pushes people towards an extreme mindset as a means of coping, leaving no room for a middle ground. The thinking becomes dichotomous: Black or white, where choices or situations are either completely good or entirely bad. In this state, one is either hypervigilant, highly alert to look for something bad to happen so that they can be prepared or become numb or detached, sort of a shutdown to protect themselves.

There is no denying that survival mode is a natural, instinctive response designed to protect us in times of danger. It brings with it heightened awareness, quick decision-making and presence of mind. The energy that comes with the survival mode is powerful, it gets dissipated and is destructive for the body when not used.

This powerful feeling can be repurposed by channelling it into activities which have a sense of purpose. Moving from a state of constant alertness, fear, and self-doubt to tremendous possibilities of growth, self-maximisation, and into a state of empowerment can happen by cultivating compassion as a state of being.

Compassion is the only superpower that can positively navigate the survival journey. It may sound gentle and soothing; however, this is what one needs when the storm of the survival instincts passes. The healing, nurturing and soothing force of compassion can calm the internal storm. With this superpower, one can navigate life with meaning, grace, and joy.

People who are conditioned to put the word in a box of a fixed definition describe compassion as a 'Concern for the sufferings of others.' This is a very narrow viewpoint that does not capture the deep understanding behind the emotion of compassion.

Compassion is much more than what popular definitions state, encompassing a deep emotional state and awareness about oneself and others' suffering, which could be physical, emotional, psychological, or spiritual discomfort or financial. It could also be about relationship adversity, hardships, traumas, or any other kind of difficulty. It goes beyond just recognising the pain, there is a genuine desire to act to ease or eliminate the suffering.

Pure altruistic actions have deep roots embedded in thinking soaked in compassion. There is an innate intention to see people around free of any suffering. This intention leads to valuing good in others, looking at life from different perspectives and hence not getting tied down with one fixed point of view, this one super power is the social glue which has and will keep humanity together.

Buddha & The Real Kingdom

The idea of compassion has been revealed to the world countless times across various religions, cultures, and races. One of the torchbearers of this transformative concept was Gautam Buddha. It is noteworthy that compassion was the superpower that transformed Siddhartha Gautama, a prince living in luxury and sheltered from harsh realities, into the world teacher, Buddha. He was not born a Buddha; he reached that state with his own effort.

Buddha is not a name; it is a title or a post. It is derived from the Pali root word "Budh", which means to "understand" or to "awake". Budh is also a Sanskrit name for the planet Jupiter, The teacher. The one who rises from the mud of ignorance and blooms like a lotus is Buddha- "The enlightened" or "The Awakened."

It is a post conferred to the one who has reached an unimaginable state of development, a state of self-realisation. Humans as a race have a path of evolution just like the mineral, plant, and animal kingdoms. This path is explained in various scriptures across cultures and religions. Akin to any organisational structure, human evolution also has a line of sight.

Every human must realise they are a contender on this path. Those who are consciously on the path to Buddha-hood go through various stages of all-around development and self-realisation. Every aspirant experiences certain levels of emotional, psychological, and spiritual development, purification, and training.

In Buddhism, the one who has entered the Dharma and received the precepts is called the Initiate. The Initiate moves on to becoming "Arhats" or "Paramhamsa". For example, Paramhansa Yogananda achieved Arhatship in his lifetime, and so did Swami Vivekananda. While sharing his knowledge, teaching the path to Buddha-hood or enlightenment and giving the sermons firsthand, Gautam Buddha's disciples became Arhats just by being receptive to his teachings. Buddha was the true community builder. The Sangha (a monastic community) was created by him to spread compassion and morally uplift society. The objective of the Arhats was to achieve their life goals by being a good example and spreading the path to enlightenment. When you are an Arhat or Paramhansa, it is no longer about oneself; the work is to uplift the clan towards the higher and the universal purpose.

Once the work at the level of an Arhat is complete, the next level requires bigger tasks, and then, one becomes a Bodhisattva before becoming a Buddha. Lord Maitreya (Which means friendship) is prophesied to become the next Buddha. His main aim again will be to awaken humanity by re-emphasising Gautam Buddha's teachings of Dharma, which have largely been forgotten. Buddha sits in living rooms or gardens as a painting or a statue; the form remains, teachings erased.

Gautam Buddha had played his part to get to the best version of a human being. He was self-realised after such suffering, struggle, heartbreak and detachment. He lived a luxurious life. His father, King Suddhodana of the Shakya clan, was foretold about the great one being born, hence he made sure to shower him with the most opulent and comfortable life such that Siddhartha (Gautam Buddha's name before the enlightenment) does not think of leaving the palace. He was protected, shielded from the world, even from the environment, even given different palaces to endure and enjoy different seasons. He was surreptitiously cut off from the real world.

However, one day, his inner calling set him off outside the palace, where he encountered four sights that forever changed the course of his life. These "Four Sights" awakened his desire to understand man's suffering and unearthed a deep state of compassion to do something about it for everyone.

The first sight - An old man

This was the first time he had observed ageing. This sight revealed that youth and physical strength are fleeting. When you have the strength of youth, accomplish an extraordinary, limitless life with meaningful experiences. Age gracefully with purpose and passion.

The second sight – A sick man

Illness, bad health (physical, emotional and mental), disease, pain, stress, financial and emotional distress are part of life's plan. It is a given, a fixed cost. Challenges, periods of crisis and obstacles are part of life's experiences.

The third sight – A corpse

The impermanence of life, the deterioration of the body and the constancy of change must be acknowledged. Pleasure and pain are both transient; life itself is not guaranteed. Hence, attachment to people, things, and clinging to material possessions is futile. When the body is lifeless, what is the use of status, designation, house, furniture, bank balance, clothes, jewellery, car, and so on?

The fourth sight- A holy man

Seeing a wandering ascetic gave Sidhartha hope and the courage to find the possibilities of rising above the suffering.

This was the turning point for Prince Siddhartha to find the root cause of suffering so that he could find the solution. He left his palace, the comfort zone, wife, child, and material possessions in the quest to find the solution. Compassion was more powerful than comfort. Compassion was longer lasting than comfort. Compassion worked like fire to do something big for the evolution of humanity.

He left his family, possessions, status, and much more to find the solution, however, they say he did not abandon humanity after leaving his body. It is said that he is still providing the spiritual energy, ideas, empowerment to the earth and patiently waiting till the last man evolves. He has the choice to move to many other universes, but his compassion for the human race is unfathomable and hence he again chooses compassion over comfort.

The Budha identified various kinds of sufferings:

1. **Physical suffering**- Diseases, injury, physical deterioration
2. **Emotional suffering**- Feelings of anger, sadness, despair, and so forth
3. **Psychological suffering**- Fear of the future, anxieties, unfulfilled desires, etc
4. **Spiritual suffering**- Disconnect with our nature, emptiness, questioning existence itself.

As Siddhartha wandered from place to place, he understood suffering yet was far away from the truth as to how to alleviate it. Seeking answers, he met teachers, sages, highly evolved religious leaders, and so on. He studied sacred texts, practiced intense meditations, denied his senses, pushed his body to an extreme-reducing it to bare bones.

He was led to believe that the answers will come when he rejects the physical comforts, food, senses, etc. He was led to believe that when he starves the body the mind will be free and the truth will be revealed. He stopped eating, almost starving himself to death, the answers yet eluded him. The extreme suffering left him weak and questioning the process.

Disheartened, yet not discouraged, he realised that enlightenment cannot be achieved with a weak body and tired mind. Feeling compassion for his body and understanding that physical fitness is important for spiritual progress, he nourished his body with coarse food.

His five close disciples, waiting for Gautama to impart the secret knowledge, felt disappointed in the change of course. They thought Gautama went back to the futile pleasure of feeding his body. When Gautama most needed the support, they left him thinking he was back in the lap of comfort.

This did not deter Gautama, who, with a polished mind and strong will, decided to develop and follow his own intuition. That is why he does not force himself on others. He encourages you to think, evaluate and make your decisions. Humanity has been marred by dogmas and fixated thinking. We need to think for ourselves. That is what is the meaning of 'What we think, we become'.

Buddha sat under the Bodhi tree for 49 days to find the truth. Every week, he was enlightened by something new, everyday his old thoughts were renewed with greater, deeper insights. In ancient Hindu texts, there is the concept of Kundalini yoga. In Kundalini, our inner energy is also said to have 49 layers, and, as each layer is developed, the mind gains access to inner truths.

Ultimately, the existing teachings and rituals only got Buddha to a certain point; after that, it was his own journey inwards. Similarly, teachers, gurus, saints, religions, rituals, etc can take you to a place where the journey, willpower, motivation, and purpose are yours. One should not stop there; each one will have a different experience, insight, and learning.

One of Buddha's greatest triumphs, and a story that perfectly illustrates the beauty of compassion, is his encounter with the dreaded murderer Angulimala. This infamous thief wore the fingers of his victims as a garland. Upon meeting Buddha, the fabled criminal was intent on violence, but Buddha's abundant, unwavering, and indiscriminate compassion transformed

Angulimala to the point where he gave up his crimes and ended up becoming a frontline figure in Buddhism.

Gautam Buddha dared to discard the old and believe in self- realisation. The path of creation is challenging, and those who believe in archaic beliefs may not come along; it can be disheartening. When what one is creating comes from a higher ground, compassion and non-individualistic, which may benefit a larger cause, one is given the playing field to move forward.

Buddha brought out the innate super power in all humans, yet not tapped because of other distractions such as: caste-system, gender roles, superstitions, oppression of the weak and downtrodden, especially the animal kingdom. He did not give sermons, rather encouraged people to think for themselves through a way of questioning or dialogue.

This takes us to a similar way of spreading the light adopted by Plato, a Greek philosopher, whose works influenced education, metaphysics, ethics, politics and philosophy. His influential and most impactful work, 'The Republic', includes 'The Allegory of the Cave', which symbolises how people live in the dark cave of ignorance. It also reflects the difficulties "The enlightened ones" face when trying to share their knowledge with others. Those who have not experienced enlightenment resist or even attack those who reveal the truth.

The Allegory of The Cave

Imagine a group of people who have been chained inside a dark cave since birth. They are facing the wall of the cave with their backs towards the mouth of the cave. They cannot see each other or the outside world. Behind these prisoners, there is a fire, which means they see other objects or other people as shadows cast on the wall. For them, shadows are the only reality.

One of the prisoners, out of great curiosity, courage and desire, breaks free and dares to step out of the cave. At first, the sun blinds him, and he is overwhelmed. Gradually, he adjusts his vision and sees reality, realising that the shadows were mere illusions.

Out of sheer compassion, the free man returns to the cave to release the other prisoners, share the truth and show them the real world. However, the other prisoners, bound by their chains and belief in the shadows, refuse to accept that there is a real world outside. They are comfortable with their truth and even get hostile or mock the freed person.

The Allegory of the Cave is an ancient quest of all enlightened beings, their responsibility to go back to the cave of ignorance and free the prisoners of shadow- perceptions, beliefs based on distorted or wrong knowledge, judgements, viewpoints, self-centred control, etc. That is what Buddha did; he is still waiting at the exit of the cave to help humanity.

The allegory is aptly represented in modern society's obsession with social media. Just as the prisoners see only shadows on the wall, social media users often encounter information that re-confirms their existing beliefs. It doesn't challenge them. Algorithms curate content to spoon-feed users just the thing they want to see, creating an echo chamber effect.

"The Allegory of the Cave" is a powerful metaphorical framework that seamlessly enumerates the age-old teachings of Buddha, namely his "Four Noble Truths".

Befriend suffering

The first noble truth is the truth of suffering (dukha). People in the cave are prisoners, trapped inside a 'make-believe' reality. The beauty of this truth is that they are unaware of being trapped, unaware they have a choice.

Similarly, this lifetime is a cave, and sufferings in the form of conflict, crisis or challenges, may it be physical, emotional, psychological, and existential, are all part of life's journey.

The first step is to recognise and be aware of this truth. No human being is devoid of this process. The second, and most crucial step, is to accept this reality and not go into a sympathetic mode, but rather fight or flight mode when life throws challenges.

This body is like a machine; it has an expiry date, it will have running and maintenance problems, it will become old and eventually stop working. The moment this aspect is driven home organically and accepted, everything else becomes lighter and easier to handle.

Dig deeper

The second noble truth is 'The cause of suffering (Samudaya)'. It prods us to not just stare, mourn, complain, or be stuck with the suffering. The suffering is inevitable, so go further and look for the cause. The current situation is an effect of the cause set out in motion in the past.

Buddha's perspective about the cause is ignorance. The people in the cave believe that the shadows are the only reality. The ignorance (Avidya), that there could be something beyond the cave, and the attachment to the shadows, is the mental, emotional, and physical bondage.

Isn't this true for most of the family belief systems, cultures, religions, cults, and nations? There is a box, and everything must fit in that box, akin to the cave. Anything outside this framework is considered 'Not appropriate' or 'Against the culture' or 'A sin.'

The attachment to transient things, cravings, anger, control, power, the same kind of pleasure repeatedly, constant complaints about the same things, and so on keep us in the loop of pain and pleasure. This cycle continues beyond this lifetime; it may have also been inherited from many lifetimes.

So, why are we attached to pain and pleasure equally? To avoid the unknown, which to the brain signals danger. Our brain naturally seeks to maintain a sense of comfort and stability. Where there is a "Comfort zone, minimum stress, and familiar settings. This is an attachment in the true sense. More of the same thing repeatedly. Stepping outside this zone requires a lot of cognitive and physical effort. This can also trigger anxiety, making the brain resist it.

The brain tries to predict future events based on past experiences due to well-established neuro-pathways. This wiring avoids unpredictable outcomes, to control the outcome, stick to what it knows and minimise errors.

Socially and culturally, sticking to the so-called man-made norms, conforming to the overarching society expectations, which is highly valued, is seen as socially acceptable and safer.

The human nature to equate the unknown with unquantifiable risk is one of the reasons to be attached to the similar patterns. This extends to control the outcome and be locked into the pattern.

The attachment to power is another cause of stagnation. Power, dominance and control are historically associated with survival. There is a mental program that those who hold physical, social, intellectual or money power have better access to success, mates, protection, and influence. Accomplishing power triggers, the reward system in the brain, dopamine is released, leading to reinforcement of the behaviour.

Non-authentic self-identity, desire to seek power, operating from a high sense of superiority, trying to do things to fit into a fixated box of norms are all ways of defence mechanisms to seek external validation. This strengthens the concept of a pre-mediated self-image, making the personality more rigid and resistant to change.

Persistent pursuit of pleasure is a program in the brain to temporarily escape from stress, pain, or discomfort. The brain attaches pleasure-seeking activities and behaviours with instant gratification of shopping, or drinking or overeating, sugar cravings, etc., as coping mechanisms to avoid deeper emotional issues. People live and die with these issues without doing anything about them. They remain in the cave, believing the attachment is life.

Harness courage

The third noble truth talks about the possibility to end the suffering (Nirodha). In "The Allegory of the Cave", the prisoner who tries to break free and realise that the shadows were mere reflections cast by the light of the sun, represents the true purpose of humans to look for the truth, which can end the suffering. Sunlight represents the light of awareness, education, wisdom, or any effort made to look for the cause, courage displayed to find the truth.

The third noble truth requires courage to find the truth. What is the source of the suffering, attachment to desire, delusions and non-commitment to self? Knowing and then letting go of these ancient habits demands awareness, understanding and courage to break free. It means bringing hope as a belief in the possibility of a better choice and then seeking the path which will help step out of the pain-pleasure cycle.

The awareness that we can break the cycle, we do not need to suffer and that we have a choice is liberating. It is the moment that we realise that destiny is not something which is pre- designed and suffering is not an unalterable fate, but a condition influenced by the misperceptions, attachments, reactions, conditioning, and habits.

This shift in perspective presents possible choices where we are not caged by pain, fears, desires or any such attachment. This understanding that we have the power to change our reality brings a sense of relief. True freedom is not to act the way we want to; it is to be free from attachments. Liberation is to consciously choose a path of not being attached to any thought, emotion, pleasure, pain, body, or any outcome.

Bhagawad Gita- Chapter 2 Verse 47:

कर्मण्येवाधिकारस्ते मा फलेषु कदाचन।

मा कर्मफलहेतुर्भूर्मा ते सङ्गोऽस्त्वकर्मणि॥

Transliteration:

"Karmanyevadhikaraste Ma Phaleshu Kadachana;
Ma Karmaphalahetur Bhur Ma Te Sangostvakarmani."

The principle of detachment is encapsulated in the concept of 'Nishkam Karma', which is the essence of the Bhagawad Gita, a concept which emphasises performing one's duty without attachment to the outcome. As we focus on the actions and detach from the action, we free ourselves from anxieties and fears of success or failure. Not just Hinduism, 'Detachment' is viewed as a universal truth across various religious, philosophical, and psychological traditions.

In Taoism, the idea of 'Wu Wei' is an approach to life that focuses on "Effortless Action." The idea is to accept one's innate strengths and nature, be content with it by using the right amount of action, the right way. This philosophy involves compassion for oneself by acting in alignment with the natural order rather than against it. The actions are with the flow of life without force or excessive efforts towards a specific desired outcome. Taoism teaches that everything in the universe operates according to its own rhythm and cycles. Wu Wei reinforces the method of being at ease, observing the natural patterns and acting in harmony with them.

Taoists use the metaphor of water to illustrate Wu Wei, which is flexible, soft, adaptable, and flowy. It can overcome the hardest obstacle by flowing over or around it, or else it can erode it with patience. There is no point in going against your nature to achieve a certain outcome; imposing too much will, it will lead to exhaustion and burnout.

Psychologists call this phenomenon the 'Flow state,' where a person is fully immersed in an activity, leading to peak performance and a sense of bliss. In the flow state, one experiences a seamless connection between one's actions and awareness. The external distractions fade away, and there is a sense of being 'in the zone'. The person, action and the object become one. There is no separation; they lose awareness of self, time, and space. Time seems to pass differently in the flow state; some feel it slowing down, while others may experience it speeding up.

The activities that induce the flow state are done with a high degree of intrinsic motivation, high levels of engagement, effortlessness and not for the sake of external rewards. Mihaly Robert Csikszentmihalyi, Hungarian American Psychologist, recognised the flow state and his research identified 'Flow' as the key factor in happiness and optimal experience.

Detachment is also emphasised as a concept in Stoic philosophy because it fundamentally relates to emotions, desires, and external circumstances. The Stoics teach that life is divided into things we can control and things we cannot. What we can control is our own thoughts, reactions, and actions. Everything else is external, such as others' perceptions, actions, external events, and, most importantly, the outcomes. Here, detachment does not mean neglect or indifference in a negative sense, but rather a rational approach to focusing on internal virtues.

Stoics believed that unending desires for wealth, pleasure, or status are the root of enslavement and unhappiness. They explained that emotions such as anger, fear, envy, etc arise from judgments about what is external.

To summarise, be unmoved by both negative and positive emotions, that is true detachment! Reaching for inner freedom is how one gains control over oneself.

Find your freedom

The fourth and final truth explains the path to end the suffering (Magga). "The Allegory of the Cave" features a prisoner who follows the sunlight outside the cave and is freed of his illusions. The light of the sun is initially blinding, but gradually, his vision adjusts to the flash, and he can see reality. He saw the truth, and out of compassion for the others, he went back to the cave to free others. However, they reject him and do not believe him, choosing to cling to their familiar shadows. Something similar happened with Buddha when he came back with the middle path, and his immediate disciples left him.

The fourth noble truth emphasises the path out of the cave, unveiling the truth through one's own efforts, discernment, and experience. Buddha does not say follow me blindly; he says follow the path according to your own understanding. Do not be blinded by authority, superstition, and knowledge. Come to your conclusions after much experimentation.

The Inner Compass

Buddha's teaching stretches far beyond the four noble truths. Buddhism talks about "The Eightfold path", a bridge that facilitates the practical application of weaving compassion into life, such that one can be free from the negative repeated patterns. The eightfold path talks about:

1. Perspective decides outcomes: Right View

The way we perceive the world is filtered through our conditioning, culture, education, belief system, and past experiences. Two people can experience the same event with completely different understanding and interpretation. This involves seeing things as they truly are, beyond illusions, judgements, biases, desire, aversion, expectation of the outcome, etc.

A good way to interpret the idea of the "Right View" is through the sport of cricket. The bowler and batter are, in principle, experiencing the same event. A few seconds ago, the batter and bowler may have exchanged a few pleasantries. Now, as the bowler marks his runup, the batter perceives the moment as an occasion to score runs, and the bowler perceives the moment as his chance to strike and pick a wicket. Same event. Different goals. The one who wins the battle between the two, is the person who can stay calm, stay objective, let go of pre-conceived notions, pre-set aversions and not get affected by the sledging.

One of the most transformative aspects of the 'Right View' step is to practice being an observer without judgement. This approach looks at happy or critical moments as clouds fading away- without the joy or stress, thoughts, or emotions. Be neutral, do not get way led by the thought or ride on it with the emotion- let it rise, drop, and pass without giving it any importance.

2. Decisions dictate results: Right Resolve

It loosely translates to the 'Right Intention'. Intention is the seed which germinates into thoughts, these generate emotions, emotions guide our speech, actions, and behaviour. Even the same action can have different outcomes depending upon the intention behind it. Right intention guides the quality of the words spoken and actions.

Actions performed with compassion, honesty and genuine care always go a long way irrespective of the outcome. This is specifically important in the scenario of feedback to the employees, instilling discipline in the children, creating personal boundaries without hurting anyone, standing up for a higher cause without feeling guilty, and so on.

Right intention is our internal GPS, and this has to be turned on specially in the time of crisis, dilemma, confusion or when there is a tug of war between right and wrong. Intention connects us with a higher purpose, further leading us to aspirations, adding a sense of meaning to the journey, instead of fighting each day.

To illustrate the importance of good intentions, let's look at the story of Dasharath Manjhi, fondly dubbed as "The Mountain Man". Manjhi's wife died in a tragic accident while climbing a mountain, and since the mountain was blocking access to the nearest hospital, she passed away without medical help. Despite pleading with the authorities time and again, the block that killed his wife was still not opened. Armed with the intention to never let this happen to anyone else, Manjhi singlehandedly carved a path through the mountain to give his village better access. One man literally broke a mountain with nothing but his good intentions. It took time, it took blood, it took sweat, but in the end, the Mountain Man finished what he set out to do.

From the perspective of psychology, intention is the starting point of the mental state and is a goal-directed behaviour. Forming an intention is vital to achieving an outcome in the way we visualise it. This further opens up the right steps to be taken. More often than not, if the intention is not right, the steps taken can be delusional, leading to somewhat of an outcome; however, it could be completely exhausting, demotivating, or requiring way too much effort. Our intention to finish a task depends upon the internal and external motivation. With a higher purpose and right intention, the task does not require extrinsic motivation. Right intention fuels intrinsic motivation to complete the task without burnout, exhaustion or mental fatigue.

Strong and clear intentions help us to maintain focus, resist distractions, and FOMO. Intention is integral to self-regulation in managing our thoughts and emotions. People are drawn to other people or products, or services that align with a long-term value and stand for a meaning. There is a shared emotional connection at a deeper level. People invest and value relationships that are trustworthy and long-lasting. Right intention brings people to a common higher ground that promotes collective interest and benefits more than one.

Compassion is the love aspect; intention is the will aspect, and directed towards a goal is intelligence. Compassionate intention in every thought is the formula to a life well lived.

3. Talk the walk: Right Speech

Mathew 15:11

"It is not what goes into the mouth that defiles a person, but what comes out of the mouth, this defiles a person"

We think of eating at the right time, in the perfect setting and relishing the meal. The meal must appeal to the senses, as we give a lot of importance to taste. So much attention is paid to the external rituals, what about the internal state? What comes out of the mouth is more important than what goes inside.

Words are a powerful reflection of a person's inner state. What goes inside the mouth is for the body, what comes out is from the heart and affects other people's mental and emotional state. Words of criticism, anger, judgment, dishonesty, gossip, idle slander, abuse, harsh, rude words, backbiting, negative perception and so on injure the personality of self and others. You cannot throw mud without dirtying your hands.

The seed of spoken words is in the thoughts. Science validates this concept. These thoughts are translated into words through cognitive and neurobiological processes. We create an internal dialogue or "Self-talk"- this influences the emotions created through the inner experiences. "Neurons that fire together wire together"-this principle of neuroscience holds that repeated thoughts create neuropathways to certain words and behaviours and eventually create habits.

According to the science of psychoneuroimmunology, negative words activate the amygdala, the brain's centre for emotions such as fear, anger, etc. These further release hormones such as cortisol, which is detrimental to physical, emotional, and mental health. A research paper from Psychological Science, the flagship journal of the Association for Psychological Science, found that negative words do end up activating the amygdala and increasing stress-related neural as well as hormonal responses.

On the contrary, positive reinforcements, self-affirmations, compassion, and journaling release dopamine and serotonin, enhancing self-worth and assurance. Behavioural neuroscience studies have gathered quantifying evidence to back the power of positivity on our mind, with one famous study implying that positive reinforcement relies critically on dopaminergic circuits.

The field of epigenetics explores how our environment, including language, influences gene health. Positive, compassionate, encouraging words build self -worth and resilience.

Quantum physics suggests that everything vibrates at a frequency, and we are all interconnected through electromagnetic waves. Hence, not just spoken words, even thoughts darted at someone can affect the sender, receiver and the environment around. A famous research paper that reviewed Quantum and Electromagnetic Fields in Our Universe and Brain, supports this view of human interconnection via waves, claiming that the brain is immersed in, and contributes to, a global electromagnetic field that, in principle, links all charged systems.

Studies by Dr Masaru Emoto on water crystals have visual validation of how positive and negative words affect the molecular structure of water. Since the human body is primarily composed of water, words may influence the body at a molecular level.

One must always remember to shift the GPS from external to internal awareness, and visualise the language and the intention behind the spoken word before it's even conceived.

Goddess Saraswati- One of the many Goddesses in Hindu tradition is a metaphor of knowledge. It is believed that one should watch out for what one speaks, because there is an auspicious time during the day when Saraswati resides on the tongue and whatever is spoken manifests.

'Saraswati' comes from the word 'Saras', which has many meanings in the Sanskrit and Hindi languages- 'Flow', 'Lake' and 'Speech'. She is depicted in the colour 'White', seated on a 'Swan'. These metaphors denote the power behind discernment between right and wrong before speaking and the purity of speech.

Ultimately, it all comes down to our words. No matter where, no matter when, always aim to practice effective, purposeful, and compassionate communication skills.

> *"Before you speak, let your words pass through 3 gates: Is it true, Is it necessary, Is it kind"*
>
> – **Rumi**

---

4. The leap that matters: Right Action

This is about what to do, when to do, and why it must be done, aligning with ethical action and balancing intention, timing and most importantly, the purpose.

It is not about overaction or inaction; it is about awareness and discernment. Overaction because of brazenness, power, pride or trying to change the outcome can lead to chaos, burnout, stress, and unnecessary conflict. Inaction can lead to stagnation, missed opportunities or injustice. Action at the wrong time could be reactive and lead to impatience, regret, or guilt.

Action with a truthful purpose is rooted in values rather than ego, fear, or societal norms. Compassionate action considers upholding the duty or the dharma and involves the welfare of everyone; it is not weak or submissive.

Inaction in the moment, born out of the intention to observe and allow the situation to unfold rather than going against the flow and forcing the outcome- this is wisdom. Surrender is a form of letting go of the need to control everything. This is a conscious choice to trust the higher order, recognise the limits of oneself and let the right thing unfold at the right time. However, inaction arising from fear of failure, fear of the unknown, fear of judgement or society norms which do not serve humanity can stunt human development and growth. The right action is rooted in purposeful intention and not emotional attachment to the outcome.

5. Do what you love to love what you do: Right Livelihood

When people choose a career which resonates with their passion, calling and innate motivation, it does not seem like work. It becomes an extension of one's purpose, aligned with the higher order and joy. This kind of activity is engaging and inherently rewarding. Research in psychology on organisational behaviour has consistently shown that employees who are motivated by their work demonstrate higher levels of productivity and are fully invested. An online article strongly backs the same belief with numbers, stating that fully motivated and engaged employees deliver 17% higher productivity and 41% lesser absenteeism.

This is living to one's highest potential and displaying self-compassion by minimising suffering in the form of discontentment. Pursuing work just for money or because it is done that way is a self injury. There is disconnection, no meaning to the duty and delusion. This slows down evolution and stagnates the mind.

The concept of choosing a career where one's passion lies can be further explored in the "Dualistic model of passion". This model prophesies that there are two kinds of passion: harmonious passion and obsessive passion. The former is a healthy practice where individuals happily internalise an activity they love, leading to flexible engagement without conflict with other life domains. The latter is an unhealthy idea where individuals use passion as an excuse to forego any sort of work-life balance.

Collective meaningful impact in the world can only happen when there is deep fulfilment in what one does. Then there is no struggle of work-life balance because that is a myth. When work looks like your purpose, everything else aligns with a greater good. There is no reinforcement that it must be ethical, non-injurious, honest, and sincere.

Money is an energy that flows with the right intention, action, and livelihood. It is a reward for courage, effort, and purpose. When you work for money, you are its slave. When you work for your own higher purpose, you are the creator. Would you like to be the creator of possibilities or a slave of uncertainty? The answer to this question will dictate the course of your career and personal life.

6. Get going: Right Effort

Life is a sacred opportunity for the soul to evolve and learn, hence each incarnation comes with a purpose. Right Effort ensures that we do not waste the gifts given to us. The mercy and love of the cosmos is that we have been given a lifeline of free will, hence we can make choices. Minerals, plants and animals do not have that gift. Their life is controlled.

Human beings can make deliberate choices to consciously engage in life and its activities that uplift the lifetime rather than diminish. They are the most intelligent beings on earth; this intelligence needs to be used for the purpose of creation, bringing more knowledge, skills, peace, and joy. The only thing they have to do is apply effort. Imagine you have been given a car with all the amenities, all you need to do is drive it.

Right effort is an invitation to humanity to commit to growth at all the levels of existence- Physical, emotional, psychological, and spiritual, recognising that growth in one area supports faster growth in another area.

At the physical level, eating healthy and balanced nutrition, sleeping well, maintaining a schedule, engaging in any form of physical activity, movement or exercise is a way to honour the body. A healthy body with emotionally turbulent feelings and thoughts is a disaster. At an emotional level it is vital to accept, acknowledge, healthily express one's emotions. At the same time, emotional restraint is equally important by not allowing emotions to dictate actions in a harmful way to oneself and others.

At a psychological level, the right effort is to develop an open, discerning and disciplined mind. Staying away from criticising people mentally is the biggest secret behind a clear and sharp mind. Learning new skills, focusing on constant self-development, going beyond the done or the comfort zone, are many such ways to keep the brain alive. Increasing the consciousness at a higher level than the current one is spiritual development. It is not about bypassing the challenges of life, but rather learning to navigate them with wisdom and developing virtues such as compassion, honesty, service, generosity, and so on.

Through constant effort, humans have the capacity to transcend their limitations and create new realities. Athletes have constantly pushed the boundaries of physical and mental endurance. 100m, marathon, and swimming records have been broken to demonstrate that the capacity of human beings is elastic and not set in stone. Previous records of climbing peaks have been shattered, with 14 of the peaks being climbed by one person over 6 months. Another record has been set by descending nearly 11000 metres to the bottom of the Mariana Trench, the deepest point in the world's oceans. Artificial Intelligence is threatening the jobs of the creators, humans, who are now looking to move to Mars.

One could delve into the inspirational story of Major D.P. Singh to understand the transformative incredulity of taking the right efforts. During the 1999 Kargil war, Major D.P. lost his right leg. Not one to be deterred by downfalls, the brave soldier turned a new leaf by training, training and training, to eventually become India's first ever blade runner. A man who was once declared dead in a hospital refused to get bogged down, took every effort to change his life, and eventually made the country proud.

Pushing human limits is our purpose, to know there are no limits, just right efforts. Technology, Artificial Intelligence and no boundary interconnected world is becoming a reality to make humans make the right efforts in the things which need attention. Technology is here to save time on mundane tasks so that we can focus on things which make us push our mental, emotional and physical self-created boundaries. A few are out there putting in efforts for the many to sit back and enjoy.

Is there another like you, exactly your face, fingerprints, iris, mindset, qualities, etc. You are unique. You have been made this way. And only the divine knows your formula. So to get to your unique self, you will have to make the right effort. That's the reason why you have been sent here. To lead the way in your unique way. There are many in your position, not all are thinking the way you are thinking. They may take time to reach where you are, by making the right efforts, you will get to your highest destination in a very short period of time.

7. Live in the now: Right Awareness

Have you heard of being 'In the moment'? When we are on autopilot and controlled by our habits, we are essentially operating in the past. When we operate out of fear or worry, conceptually, we are creating a future which could be far more positive than we are creating. This seventh pillar is a culmination of all the previous pillars and preparation for going within.

Most of the time people understand that detachment is a great idea, but they don't know how to practice it in real life. The answer is, by cultivating 'Awareness.' It is truly to be able to see the present in the context of past and future- it's like collapsing time and space, a concept which is known as 'Nothingness', 'Shunya' or 'Oneness'. This can also be understood by the commonly misunderstood concept of 'Consciousness.'

Awareness is a tool of consciousness that facilitates recognition of oneself (Self-Awareness), thoughts, words, actions, past, present, future, the surrounding world, and so on. It is being aware or being present at a particular state or all the states at the same time, which is oneness, seeing yourself not separate from the world around you. It is not linear, rather a matrix of sorts, and wherever one's awareness is fixed, that gets magnified. The experiences are stored in the conscious, dream or subconscious states; awareness is a tool to access those files from various states. Interestingly, a paper by Wamsley & Stick gold, published in 2013, titled "Dreaming, waking conscious experience, and the resting brain", shows that during both REM (Rapid Eye Movement) dreaming and resting wakefulness, our recent experiences are replayed to strengthen and reorganise memories for future use.

If we know that what we are accessing is just an experience of the past or a possible consequence in the future created by the awareness, there is a possibility to train oneself to look at everything from a bird's eye perspective, such that everything is subject to change, nothing is permanent. Also, our present is an effect of our past or thinking of the future. This understanding will empower and not overwhelm us.

Awareness is about being aware of oneself- inner state, external world, people, situations, environment, things. One of the ways to practice awareness is the method of 'Mindfulness'.

It is a tool to train and harness awareness in a sharper sense. It is a focused lens used to understand the small, tiny bit of the experience before labelling it as 'Good' or 'Bad' or dumping it in a negative or positive emotion bag in the subconscious closet.

Our sense of awareness is heightened when one is mindful of every thought, observes it objectively without judgment, bias or prejudice as a third person, understands the emotion attached to it, can feel this emotion creating a certain charge in the body, which subsequently leads to repeated tendencies, habits and patterns. This heightened degree of sensitivity at the level of the body, feeling, emotion and thought makes one act on one's detachment from unwanted thoughts, emotions and regulate them.

As we work on developing awareness, eventually, one can reach a state where there is no separation between self and the outside, transcending physical, emotional and mental realms, getting into a state which is beyond time and space.

Awareness is further supported by a special construct. Some call it the sixth sense, a few call it clairvoyance, but it is actually a very simple yet powerful feeling, commonly called intuition.

1. **The might of intuition**: In the book 'Autobiography of a Yogi', Paramhamsa Yogananda presents numerous anecdotes of saints and yogis who demonstrated what is known as omnipresence or the ability to be present at multiple places and interact with many people at the same time. He describes these abilities not as miracles, but as a progressive outcome of years of practice of expanding the awareness. Consciousness

is not bound by the linear progression of time or physical distance or boundaries. This is exactly the framework in quantum physics. The expansion of consciousness is the secret behind developing intuition.

a. Intuition is the ability to understand something without the need for conscious reasoning, knowledge or prior information. It is not a 'gut feeling', which develops with experience or prior knowledge. Intuition has worked in many fields such as science, business, medicine, and personal decision-making, etc
b. Steve Jobs often spoke about intuition in his decision-making process. Most of his decisions had been unconventional and ahead of their time. Oprah Winfrey credits much of her transformation to intuition. Albert Einstein believed in intuition behind key scientific discoveries and famously said, "The only really valuable thing is intuition" Vincent Van Gogh's famous piece "The Starry Night", has an uncanny resemblance to images of the spiral galaxies like the Whirlpool Galaxy, captured by the Hubble Space Telescope almost 100 years after the masterpiece was painted.
c. Sri Yukteshwar Giri, Paramhamsa Yogananda's guru, in his book 'The Holy Science' (1894) revealed the concept of 'Yugas' or cyclical ages humanity has been going through, influenced by the movement of the sun around a dual star in the solar system. He suggested that the sun revolves around a grand centre or a dual star, and this takes about 24000 years to complete, which affects the consciousness of humanity. Satya yuga was when the sun was closest to

the centre. As the sun moved away, the Kali yug began, leading to lower ages. All this precision without the scientific instruments! Modern astronomy has confirmed that the sun is not stationary; it moves around the centre of the Milky Way galaxy takes a 'Galactic year' (225-250 million years) to complete one full orbit.

d. Despite being a householder, Sri Yuketeshwar Giri was an advanced practitioner of the path of Dharana and Dhyaan laid down in the Yoga Sutras of the great saint Patanjali. After his disciplined approach and many years of Sadhana, he followed a unique approach to integrate science into spirituality. The time had come for humanity to practice spirituality with a scientific approach, such that there is authenticity and no superstitions or blind faith. He was able to connect easily between the conscious and superconscious state.

2. **Wonders of the vagus**: The secret code to understand intuition lies in our heart, and that is through compassion. A significant part here is played by the 'Vagus nerve', which is the longest cranial nerve in the body, extending from the brain stem (Medulla Oblongota) down to the abdomen. It facilitates two-way communication between the brain and the heart, and vice versa.

   a. Studies establish that about 4-in-5 of the Vagus nerve's fibres send information from the body up to the brain, while roughly 1-in-5 carry commands from the brain down to the body. From the neck, small branches of the vagus reach the heart, connect with the heart's own tiny nerve network, and then spread to the body's natural pacemaker (sino-atrial node), the atrio-ventricular node, and the heart muscle itself.

b. The above facts make it evident that the Vagus nerve plays a vital role in transmitting the sensations of the intuition from the superconscious state to the heart and the brain, so that these sensations make sense and the brain can process them consciously. That is why, when your heart feels something deeply, you want to act on it. Since the vagus nerve also extends to the gut, it is referred to as the "gut feeling".
c. The intuition from the superconscious state through the medulla oblongata is sent to the heart first, then to the brain, for it to make sense and act on it. If the heart is not full of compassion and empathy, this sensation dies out, and hence, it does not get registered fully.
d. An in-depth study published in Alternative Therapies in Health and Medicine found that the heart does indeed appear to receive and respond to intuitive information, with significantly greater heart rate deceleration occurring before future emotional stimuli compared to calm stimuli.
e. For our intuition gears to be well-oiled, compassion keeps the body in the parasympathetic state, where it is more receptive to subtle intuitive signals. One can hear and trust the inner guidance. The vagus nerve further plays a vital role in integrating emotional and cognitive responses, allowing the intuitive guidance to feel 'True' and aligned.

3. **The ills of self-doubt**: A self-doubting, critical, fearful and judgmental mind creates turbulent waves, which interfere with the intuitive signals, taking the neuro pathways to negative experiences. This may automatically reject intuitive signals as invalid or irrelevant. Judgmental or critical thinking can alter the neural pathways, reinforcing patterns of negative self-assessment, focusing more on external validation rather than listening to one's inner voice.
    a. This may, in turn, cause a person's self-esteem to dive. Medical evidence reflects that when people with low self-esteem hear criticism, three brain "alarm" centres overreact: the anterior cingulate cortex (ACC) flags errors, the medial prefrontal cortex (mPFC) reinforces "I'm not good enough" thoughts, and the anterior insula heightens that gut-wrenching feeling, together making negative feedback feel much worse.
    b. This is where most people get stuck, managing their self-esteem, self-worth or self-image. The inner voice is subdued or suppressed when one is constantly evaluating basic success or failure. When the source of validation is external, the heart is not talking; the cognitive function is taking the lead.
4. **The importance of self-compassion**: Self-compassion can build a nurturing inner environment for intuition to flourish. Kirsten Neff is a pioneering researcher in this field. Neff's overview notes that practising self-compassion "fosters a nurturing inner environment that allows personal insight and growth to unfold". She has extensively studied, researched,

and written about self-compassion. Her work highlights three components of Self-Compassion, namely:

a. Self-Kindness vs Self-judgement: First, direct the kindness inwards, towards yourself, which you will eventually offer to others. Don't be harshly critical or judgmental. The world is out there. When you show kindness to yourself, it will flow to others and will be reciprocated.
b. Common Humanity vs Isolation- This is the acceptance that you are not alone, everyone makes mistakes and experiences difficulties, which is part of being interconnected and a shared human experience, hence not an isolated self-inadequate one
c. Mindfulness vs Over-identification- This refers to observing, acknowledging, accepting, and holding your thoughts and emotions rather than ignoring them or becoming overwhelmed with them.
d. Self-compassion should not be misunderstood as Self-pity, Self-indulgence or a weakness. It builds self-resilience, courage, and a relationship with oneself. Compassion begins with oneself, especially in cultures that glorify overextending and overworking. Ruthless individuals often lack self-compassion due to the stories they have heard, seen and gone through in the growing up years. Success and leadership are traditionally equated with toughness, dominance, and control. A man who shows any sign of vulnerability is judged as not being man enough. As the ruthless behaviour is consistently rewarded by things getting done faster, it remains an easy habit when things need to be in control.

e. Self-compassion requires more work; it needs courage and stepping out of the unfamiliar to reevaluate the stereotypical success matrix, to look at the long-term horizon where there is rest, recovery, reassessment and no burnout or hustle culture. Right awareness begins with being compassionate towards ourselves.
f. The price of lack of self-compassion is heavy. Some forms of cancer, autoimmune diseases, and mental health conditions can be attributed to subjecting the cells to negative, critical, self-debilitating thoughts of neglect, worthlessness and low confidence. So, whatever you do in life, wherever you are in life, never give up being kind to yourself.

8. Eye of the tiger: Right Concentration

Going back in time, there's a famous anecdote from the Mahabharata, about a competition where all the suitors for the queen had to pass a test by stringing a mighty bow, and shooting an arrow to pierce the eye of a rotating wooden fish mounted high above. The competitors could only look at the fish's reflection in the pool of water below. While many tried and failed, it was Arjuna who was successful in achieving this feat. When asked by his teacher, Dronacharya, Arjuna answered that he could see only the eye of the fish.

The "eye of the fish" in the reflection of the water symbolically is loaded with many secrets. It represents the nature of the human being incarnated in the body, living through the lower mind and emotions. The real fish and the reflection represent the duality of nature; the body is just the reflection of the higher self or the higher soul. Illusions, distractions, and emotions mislead us from the path. Rotation of the fish, the lower mind, is always distracted and turbulent with thoughts seen through the emotions represented by water.

Understanding over judgment

Rakesh, a manager in a start-up, had an intern who kept missing deadlines. Frustrated, he was ready to fire her. Instead of lashing out, he paused long enough to ask, "What's going on? This is not her usual self"

The next day, he gently asked the intern, and the intern broke down: she was juggling long shifts and taking care of her ailing mother, and barely sleeping. Rakesh chose to overcome the inner critic and be a supporter. He adjusted her workload and mentored her. Within weeks, her performance improved. More importantly, she never forgot that someone saw her as a person before a resource. She became the most trustworthy person in the team.

Within this matrix of separation, how does one find the centre? "The eye of the fish" is the password to the treasure, single-pointed focus. With sight on the purpose, detachment from distractions, emotional balance, senses and mind aligned, piercing through the turbulence of the outside expectations, releasing the arrow when there is complete stillness, this is the highest version of concentration with awareness.

As they say, 'When the disciple is ready, the teacher appears', Arjuna was the disciple who was chosen by Krishna for his power of awareness, concentration, courage, surrender and receptivity.

There is a rich overlap between the concepts in different religions and the teachings. The Ashtanga Yoga, or the Eight Limbs of Yoga (Union with the Higher Self), outlined by Patanjali in the Yoga Sutras, provides a similar, comprehensive path to balance physical, emotional, psychological and spiritual alignment.

1. **Yama** – The core values which help us navigate our personal and professional life, whether through managing internal or external conflict, relationships, work, self-compassion, etc.
    - **Ahimsa**: Non-harmful actions such as physical, emotional and mental injury to self and others. Eg. Guilt, harsh criticism, conceit, and jealousy all forms of emotional or psychological injury to self and others. Conscious thought of avoiding pain to others.
    - **Satya**: Speaking the truth with empathy with a higher purpose to be authentic and trustworthy.
    - **Asteya**: Refraining from stealing physically and emotionally. Giving the right due at the right time. Respecting others' time, opinion and energy. Also, not wasting one's time
    - **Brahmacharya**: Practising self-control and moderation in every aspect of life, specifically desires and habits (social media consumption, eating, spending, partying, etc). This is a misunderstood concept. Self- control pertains to conserving our life- energy, or prana, as it is called. Energy cannot be created or destroyed; it can be transmuted to something higher or lower, or it can be channelled into activities, thoughts which are productive and purposeful. Refraining from unnecessary arguments, unhealthy

eating, over-binging on media, over-drinking alcohol or unproductive, unhealthy negative thinking, etc are signs of self-control. Real freedom is that of the mind, which comes from self-control through discernment. Everyone has limited energy, and they can decide how to maximise the output.

- **Aparigraha**: Non-attachment to the outcome, letting go of a scarcity mindset, greed, and material possessions as validation of self-esteem. When there is a larger purpose, however, the focus is on the action to be taken; the outcome can be any. There are many possibilities and choices which we cannot fathom; all we need to do is focus on the baby steps and the joyful experience of getting there.
- **Niyama**: Essential self-discipline habits
- **Saucha**: Keep the body, emotions, thoughts, energy and surroundings clean and hygienic. Like attracts like; clean mental and physical energy will attract magnetism and good luck.
- **Santosha**: Develop an "abundance mindset", be in the present moment, be grateful for everything, celebrate others' success. The belief that there is scarcity of resources, hoard money, lack of good things in life, uncertainty of future in terms of money or opportunities, leads to an overall pessimistic mindset, not allowing the human to breach his limitations.
- **Tapas**: Develop willpower through the right diet, exercise, thinking positively, and refraining from dumping unhealthy food, emotions and thoughts in the body and

mind. Willpower, smart work and consistent effort are the basic ingredients of success.

- **Svadhyaya**: Self-awareness by inner reflection to develop one's abilities of compassion, sensitivity, and concentration. There is no one coming to save you; self-work and effort can take you out of the ditch of darkness.

2. **Asana**: Yoga means union, and it begins with keeping the body healthy. Body positivity through healthy eating and physical fitness is the basic requirement to control the body through flexibility, strength, and better posture. The fitness fever is slowly being taken seriously, and there is more information available about most of the chronic diseases rooted in a sedentary and unhealthy lifestyle.

3. **Pranayama**: The concept of controlling the life force through breath regulation is slowly getting its due. Various breathing techniques are now widely recognised by sports scientists and life coaches to shift from sympathetic to parasympathetic mode, calm the nervous system, enhance focus, and enhance immunity. Deep abdominal breathing techniques with a hold, popularly known as 'Box' Breathing, have a vital impact in bringing down anxiety and enhancing the quality of sleep. Our breath is the link between the physical, emotional, and mental aspects of the body. The technique of becoming aware of the breath, its movement, rhythm, balance between inhalation and exhalation, slowing it down, breathing in and out from the abdomen, has a calming effect on the brain; unnecessary thoughts vanish, the entire body gets charged. This prepares

us to detach from the outside world and bring attention to the inner consciousness.

4. **Pratyahara**: Once the body is relaxed and the mind detached from the outside world, the focus is to further raise the consciousness from the lower, everyday, mundane life. In today's digital age where social media has invaded private time and distractions are way too many, conscious disconnection from giving the senses wasteful, short-lived pleasure is important. Intermittent fasting, digital detox, silent retreats, holding the breath, refraining from sugars, vegetarian/vegan/gluten-free diets, conscious clothing, etc are modern techniques of Pratyahara.
   - True strength is not merely to be the best or the ability to defeat others, but rather to master one's own thoughts and emotions. Making the right choice in any given moment is the ability to understand whether one is avoiding a situation because of pain, or repeating a certain pattern because of the momentary pleasure and escaping from pain. This understanding eventually leads to the withdrawal of awareness from the senses at will. It's all about finding the balance by conscious withdrawal from the outside world, which has encroached our bedrooms through devices and selective engagement in activities which are uplifting.
   - We live in a world where Artificial Intelligence is personalising experiences of learning, proactive problem-solving, quick decision making, reducing uncertainty, helping save time on micro-tasks, saving tremendous time and easing the brain to think. The other side of the digital

rainbow is constant connectivity, blurring lines between self and outside. The information overload is causing brain fatigue, and the algorithms are designed to capture and retain attention, leading to a fragmented attention span. Humans are becoming lazy, boxed and losing connection with the real world. Decreasing attention to intuition is depleting human agency, critical thinking skills and loss of confidence in one's judgement.

- There is immense merit in constantly utilising human skill and mental instinct, even if advanced technology may lead us to believe otherwise. Let's examine the case of London's eponymous cab drivers, fondly known as cabbies. These drivers go through rigorous mental training to study, memorise and undertake countless hours of 'Run' of London streets and alleys. The aforementioned practice takes about 3-4 years to master the routes. This requires a high level of mental spatial memory and mental flexibility as the cognitive maps are created in the brain, and the connection between roads and places. Studies have shown that this intense method leads to structural changes in the brain.
- On the other hand, while GPS navigation has made travelling far more convenient, faster and easier, there is a growing concern among neuroscientists and psychologists that over-reliance on GPS can make parts of the brain redundant and under-utilised, pretty much the way certain species become extinct. Weekend sense of direction and lack of challenge leads to a dull mind and no intuition. Reduced

engagement with parts of the brain may have implications for cognitive ageing, memory disorders such as Alzheimer's.

- How can one keep their concentration skills sharp and smooth? Attention Restoration Therapy is a psychological theory that explains how exposure to natural environments can help restore depleted cognitive resources, particularly attention. Daily activities require effort and focus, which is directed attention, whereas 'Soft Fascination' is a concept of effortless attention that is naturally drawn to stimuli without conscious effort. Time spent in restorative environments can stimulate creativity, innovation, and a calmer mind. This environment can be created in urban planning for the physical surroundings with greener landscapes, waterfalls, sounds of birds chirping, incense, calming music, also with active meditation, chanting and breathing practices for the mind.
- Pomodoro is another technique which helps in focusing on a single task for a set period with short breaks in the middle, usually 25 minutes and short breaks for 5-10 minutes (25 minutes x 4 times). This technique encourages structuring the time between work-rest such that there is discipline, increased will power, productivity, and the rest period allows relaxation, fuelling the motivation for the next 25 minutes.
- Pratyahara is a way to manage sensory overload and cultivate control over the mind voluntarily. It is also a preparation for concentration and focus.

Pause without blame

We've all had days in the office when nothing is going right. Meena, a young lawyer, had just lost her first big case. The courtroom defeat replayed in her mind like a loop: "I'm not cut out for this. I'm a failure."

She was about to resign from her firm when her mentor asked her one simple thing: "If your closest friend were in your place, would you speak to her the way you're speaking to yourself?" That question broke her spiral. That night, instead of berating herself, she wrote: "I did my best. I'm still learning. It's okay to stumble." Compassion for herself gave her space to try again. Months later, she stood in court again- steadier this time.

5. **Dharana**- This refers to 'Right Concentration' in Buddhism's Eight-Fold Path. Concentration is focused on a particular object, stemming from the idea that what you give your attention to grows. This is tied to the power of manifestation as energy flows to where you put your attention. The Reticular Activating System in the brain plays the key role here – It filters information and influences what we notice and pay attention to. When we think about something (Positive or negative), our brain throws out unrelated information and amplifies anything that supports our focus. This leads to confirmation bias. When we focus on self-compassion over perfection, we nourish our goals and purpose.

6. **Dhyaan**- After having substantial control over the body, calming the mind, bringing it to one point of attention, one needs to prolong the focus on that point. The 'Monkey

Mind' will keep hopping from one mundane and unnecessary thought to another; we cannot stop the mind from thinking and creating flutter, that is what it feeds on. However, the prolonged practice of pratyahara enables the mind to focus on that one point for a longer period to master the technique. Professionals in Surgery, sports, creative arts, baking, software coding and so on, enter a heightened state of awareness and must focus on the tasks for a long period of time. This is a state of dynamic stillness when the mind is calm and clear, the body is active, and they almost know what's coming.

7. **Samadhi**- This is the modern-day flow state where one loses the sense of self, and consciousness expands to an extent where there is unity and timelessness. This state can be developed by adapting the Eightfold Path or the Yoga Sutras of Patanjali.

   Compassion is the superpower which is essential for reaching higher states of consciousness, samadhi or a flow state where there is effortlessness in the task, joy in every action, even if it is the most strenuous or painstaking job.

Being the better half

It's late, and your partner snaps at you over something small. Perhaps the dishes or a forgotten errand. The reflex is to push back: "So what if I didn't? Why are you always so moody?" But compassion notices the tiredness in their eyes, the weight of their day. Instead of escalating, you respond softly: "Don't worry about the dishes, I'll make up for it, I'll take over them for the rest of the week! But is something stressing you out? Is there something bugging you from inside?" That one question changes the evening. A fight dissolves into a heartfelt conversation about work pressures and hidden worries. By choosing compassion over defensiveness, you deepen connection instead of widening the gap.

The Brahmaviharas or "The Four Divine Abodes", are the essential qualities defining compassion.

1. **Metta (Loving-Kindness)**: Developing the heart towards love that does not expect anything in return. This stems from being grateful for everything and understanding the space from where others may be coming.
2. **Karuna (Compassion)**: Genuine purpose towards the higher good, to see everyone as a child of God and work towards alleviating suffering. There is a dharma of humanity towards the incarnation- to make it large, purposeful and maximum.
3. **Mudita (Sympathetic Joy)**: Deriving joy in the happiness and success of others. This is an answer to moving from a scarcity mentality to an abundant state of mind.
4. **Upekkha (Equanimity)**: A balanced and unbiased state of calm, still and centred in the wake of both ups and downs. This is maintaining grace and a detached perspective towards pain and pleasure because both are fleeting.

It is easier said than done, in this world with overwhelming information, there are a few tools to guide for developing compassion. Meditation on Loving-Kindness or the Twin Hearts Meditation is a development by Grand Master Choa Kok Sui, founder of Arhatic Yoga; The most advanced spiritual technology to achieve expansion of consciousness, transcend the physical limitation and connect with the higher self.

This meditation is designed to address the challenges of modern times, such as time limitations to develop the inner self, lack of stillness and calm, external noise, and so on. It doesn't have any prerequisites. It is simple, easy to comprehend and straightforward practice. Being a guided meditation, it leaves nothing for the practitioner to figure out on their own. The short technique rapidly stimulates the key energy centres in the body, which are crucial for developing compassion and intuition.

Studies conducted on the effects of this meditation show a significant anxiety reduction and stress in novice practitioners and a reduction in depression in regular practitioners. Physiological parameters suggest a notable reduction in blood pressure, improvements in heart rate variability and potential benefits in cardiovascular health. Neuropsychological studies indicate better memory, clarity of mind, and emotional regulation. Practitioners also fare better at decision-making and report heightened intuition. EEG studies have shown that the Twin Hearts Meditation can lead to an increase in alpha and theta brainwave activity. Alpha waves are associated with a relaxed yet more aware state, while theta waves are linked to deep relaxation, creativity, and intuition. The sleep is more restorative and deeper.

Compassion is the superpower that transcends the boundaries of everyday mundane human limitations. It carries with itself the boundless force that connects us to the deeper truths of shared humanity. Compassion invites us to see beyond the ordinary, lowly, and mediocre illusions that do not let us rise -judgments, fears, hurts, love lost, ego, jealousy, pride,

Choosing compassion is about breaking free from the grip of ordinary living and tapping into the infinite pool of free-flowing knowledge without having to prove the outcome. It is a surge of immense strength that breaks the walls of limitations and be that part of something larger, interconnected waves of goodness that can change the world around.

Kindness in the Everyday

Not just on a spiritual, philosophical or psychological level, compassion is the gift that can illuminate our daily lives in the simplest of ways possible. It could be in the workplace, on the street or at home; compassion can help us steer our everyday life with ease, too.

Easing the cycle

Anjali often clashed with her teenage son. Every small disagreement spiralled into shouting matches. She felt disrespected; he felt misunderstood. One evening, after a particularly heated argument, Anjali paused. Instead of focusing on his words, she looked at his face — red, tired, overwhelmed. For the first time, she asked herself, "What if he's not trying to fight me, but fighting something inside him?"

The next morning, instead of another lecture, she quietly said, "I can see you're stressed. It must be hard to handle school pressure and my expectations at the same time. I'm sorry I've only been scolding instead of listening." Her son, stunned, softened. He admitted he feared failing his exams and didn't know how to ask for help. That moment of compassion didn't solve all conflicts overnight, but it broke the cycle of hurt. Their conversations slowly shifted from confrontation to collaboration. Compassion in the family doesn't mean ignoring mistakes; it means choosing to know and understand the perspective over escalation.

These compassion hacks may not apply to every person, or to every situation, but the core idea here is that, in most places in life, acting with compassion might just make things brighter and better. To each their own, and you are the best judge of when to be compassionate and when to be pragmatic, but a balance of the two, with more emphasis on compassion, is one of the ways to keep our inner happiness intact.

Law of gravity…is the Law of Compassion

You cannot see gravity, you can feel it; it keeps the feet to the ground, holds mountains and oceans to the earth, it is an invisible power holding everything together. What gravity is to the physical world, compassion is to the emotional world. It pulls people toward each other, grounds them in humanity, binds families, teams, nations, and societies.

Compassion is the original GPS running in the fabric of creation. It is the reason trees give shade, rivers flow, and the body manages itself. The heart doesn't say, "I have pumped enough blood, now I need to rest", and lungs don't judge the brain for consuming more oxygen.

The most long lasting super power is not domination, it is connecting people. When you act with compassion and larger benefit- not to forget your own- you hack into a higher operating system. And you ask yourself- What is possible for the team, unit or us- rather what is in it for me. That is when more ideas, intuition and support come through. You would notice- most who look out for themselves may reach the top too fast, too soon, and do not remain there for long.

In the age of algorithms, humanity must turn to compassion to find the competitive edge and cooperation. It begins with the self, just like trees, roots take the nutrients, nourish the tree before bearing fruit and offering to others.

Once you have embraced gratitude and imbued compassion into the core of your very being, you are ready to uncover the magnanimous might of the next power.

The Third
Super Power

FORGIVENESS

The Paradox We Live With

Why do we need to forgive? Have we ever looked into this? The reason forgiving is necessary is that it is the only way to unveil our raw, hard and negative emotions that need to be freed. What are those emotions? Let us go on a small reading journey to find out.

We inhabit a paradoxical world, where contradictions coexist to shape our experiences. Technological breakthroughs have connected us like never before, entered our bedrooms and washrooms, allowing instantaneous communication even in the remotest parts of the globe. Yet, despite these so-called advancements, more people feel isolated and lonely. We are digitally connected but emotionally isolated.

Scholars have also coined a term for this, labelling it as the 'Disembodied Disconnect', where more and more digital interactions are causing fewer and fewer humans to actually connect in the offline world, essentially eliminating many physical dynamics necessary for maintaining human bonding.

Not only that, but this increasing mental dependence on social media and the virtual world is threatening our sense of individual thinking. We are moving more and more towards growing into a hive mind society, and that may not be a good development. In this case, it is more of a digital hive mind, one where shared thinking that bonds and speeds coordination online, but, more worryingly, it nudges herd mentality, subtly dulling independent judgment and nuance.

A hive-minded behaviour amplifies herd effects and weaker independent judgment, especially online. Some philosophers warn that rising digital interconnection may be steering society toward hive-mindedness or even a shared consciousness, raising hard questions about free will and whether individuality can persist as collaboration and brain-to-net interfaces intensify.

As a species, we may be inclined to find scientific depth behind everything, but we are superficial in going deep in connecting with humans. We know more, yet we fear strangers. There is proximity due to infrastructure, knowledge, sharing, and yet, genuine interaction fades into ghosting and misunderstanding. Physically, we are closer, we're all over.

We live in a world where the quintessential definition of success is a chase to gain material wealth rather than living with a sense of purpose. The means to generate wealth have remained constant through the centuries. There are endless groups and communities online, yet less love in society, countless achievements to show off on LinkedIn, yet less fulfilment in our minds, a spate of activism all around, yet less inclusion when and where it matters.

The core of the paradox of self is the eluding of authentic identity and the desire to conform. The moulds of roles are so strong and rigid, aligning to some misplaced standards of acceptance, belonging and success that there is no sense of a unique self anymore. The fragmented sense of self struggles when an individual is torn between who they genuinely are and who they wish to be perceived to be.

As humans, the paradox of self is intricately linked to our evolving nature. We are not meant to be static, influenced by different experiences, relationships and environments, we need to embrace dynamism. Lack of acceptance of change or fluidity creates conflicts.

Paradoxes are real and fascinating; they challenge the way we think. Life is not black or white; that is what polarities reveal- the grey areas. Thinking in extremes leaves a large part unanswered, and with a limited perspective, it makes no sense. This grey land is bumpy and unclear, like trying to fit water in a certain shape. It is a fertile land for creating erroneous thoughts, which are known as cognitive distortions. Humans don't know how to deal with complications, hence keep everything stark and simple so that they don't have to face failure or disappointments.

Society's lopsided perceptions may stem from cognitive distortions. Cognitive distortions, or erroneous thoughts, were first identified by Psychiatrist Dr Aron T. Beck in the 1960s, and he is regarded as the father of Cognitive Behavioural Therapy. These misrepresented thoughts have a huge impact on self-talk because they distort how one interprets the events, the personal abilities and even self-worth. The inner voice turns into a harsh critic rather than a supportive guide.

Building on Beck's work, psychologist Dr David D. Burns made the concept more accessible to people. In Burns' reinterpretation, some common types of misrepresentation of reality leading to cognitive distortions are as follows:

1. All-or-Nothing Thinking

Viewing things in extremes, black or white, is a dangerous way of looking at life. It is lazy thinking since it is easy for the human mind to create boxes or labels to put their thoughts in, and then extract feelings out of it: May it be good/bad, easy/difficult, beautiful/ugly, interesting/boring, strong/weak and so on. It is our obsession to compare or find a label to describe things.

For example, "I am such a failure, haven't been able to lose 2kgs in a week, I need to be successful at everything I do, otherwise I am a failure".

2. Overgeneralisation

Focusing on one piece of information and making conclusions based on that. It is an assumption that one negative event or outcome will lead to subsequent events that will be negative too. For example, a negative experience in one relationship may lead to the false belief that one is not lucky or good enough in relationships.

A single event can turn into a broad negative narrative- "This always happens to me".

3. Mental Filtering

As humans, our upbringing is largely based on the need to always be perfect or strive to be as close to perfect as possible. We use criticism as a tool to motivate. What a lot of us actually don't realise is that thoughts are thoughts, they are neutral! They get charged negatively or positively when feelings are attached to them. These feelings show up in the body and eventually in the behaviour. Filtering out positives and magnifying the negatives is distorted thinking. Invalidating the positives prevents one from thinking clearly.

For example, when an employee dwells on negative feedback rather than looking at many things that are working, thinking "I messed up that one little detail", he is actually ignoring all the hard work and things that he did right.

4. Jumping to conclusions

Repeated patterns make individuals slaves of the past. Assumptions based on outcomes and without any solid evidence make people jump to conclusions. Mind reading into others' actions or intentions and interpreting them according to one's filter of judgment is distorted thinking. Another possibility is when one tries to predict the outcome of a situation out of fear, doubt or past negative experiences. There is no actual evidence to prove the outcome.

For example, when you meet someone, and they are preoccupied with some other thoughts, you jump to the conclusion that they don't like you. You start thinking "They must feel I am incompetent", setting yourself up for stress which does not exist.

5. Catastrophizing

When you focus on a small part of an event and magnify it disproportionately, it causes a negative domino effect.

Instead of looking at the bigger picture, which may be quite promising and bright, you focus on one dark spot and become obsessed with it, till that's all you see.

For example, some people always operate with preconceived effects of worst-case scenarios while reaching a goal, just to be prepared. Whereas, there could be more positive chances of ease and success. All it takes is for someone to spill coffee, and in your mind, the entire day is jinxed.

6. Personalisation

Some people have the tendency of burdening themselves by taking everything personally. Such people usually feel it is their fault for things which are not even in their control. Carrying the backpack of responsibility and guilt.

For example, if a flight is unexpectedly delayed, and you end up being late to a place, you may end up blaming yourself and feeling it is your mistake. Whereas the fact is that you had nothing to do with the flight's extended schedule.

7. Should statements

Rules are created by humans to be in power or control. Again, it has both spectrums. 'Should statements' are invisible rules we create to keep us in a box, stuck with a label of stereotype of conformity.

Life doesn't understand rules; we don't have a prefixed standard operating rule book program in our brain- it is planted, and we believe it, follow it, till we have no idea why we are frustrated.

For example, societal notions such as "Girls shouldn't talk aloud" and "Boys should be strong" are rudimentary mandates set to define what a particular gender can and can't do. Invisible rules.

8. Emotional Reasoning

If our feelings were an accurate perception of our reality, then the entire world would be emotionally charged. Feelings are created by thoughts, and some inaccurate thoughts can create misplaced feelings. If you feel anxious about something, it doesn't make the thing wrong or when you feel good about something, it doesn't make it right.

For example, you may feel anxious while travelling in an aeroplane or feel happy while consuming dangerous drugs. While the former is a totally normal mode of transport, the abuse of the latter has ruined lives. Hence, how we feel isn't always the best indicator of a thing's value.

No matter what kind, erroneous thoughts are dangerous, as they make self-talk overly critical, negative, and inaccurate. They shift the situation to a damaging and limiting perspective.

Imagine living such a life built on lies- where the foundation of how you see yourself, others and the world is shaped by distorted beliefs, false narratives. You have convinced yourself subconsciously that you are unworthy, not good enough, incapable, unloved or less, because of some distorted thoughts. And now they are so ingrained within you that it feels like the only truth. These thoughts are holding you back from genuine connections and opportunities. You are comfortable in living smaller than your potential, settling for less because deep down there is a lie that has convinced you – this is all you deserve.

How many of us remember the age-old fairytale of The Ugly Duckling? The poor little duckling is constantly led to believe it is undesirable and unworthy. But, by the end, he not only finds a group where he is warmly accepted, but also realises he is nothing like how the world made him out to be. He was much more than the labels he had put on himself. He was not an ugly duckling.

The Many Faces of Our Emotions

"What you see in others is a reflection of yourself"

– Rumi

What we see around us mirrors what is happening within us. When we see beauty, kindness, or love in someone else, it's because we focus on the same qualities existing within us. Conversely, when we find faults, negativity or anger in others, we are revealing unresolved feelings or issues inside ourselves.

Science and society underscore the value of emotional awareness for physical, mental, and relational health. Interestingly, it is the same science that also suggests that a significant population struggles with emotional awareness. Psychologists have typically named this condition- Alexithymia- a condition characterised by difficulty in recognising and describing emotions.

A 2014 study by Dr Lisa Feldman Barrett, a leading researcher in affective neuroscience, found that an average person has difficulty distinguishing emotions such as anger, frustration, or anxiety. Her research points out that while people experience a vague sense of feeling bad or good, they lack the ability to pinpoint exactly what they are feeling.

Barrett's research shows that emotional granularity- the ability to label emotions- is associated with better mental health and regulation of emotions. People with low emotional granularity (Who can only identify broad emotions like 'happy' or 'sad') often struggle with anxiety and depression because they cannot address their emotions effectively.

A comprehensive study by Equanima.io found that nearly two-thirds of people are not fully aware of their emotions as they experience them, hence, they are more likely to act impulsively, experience higher stress levels, and struggle with relationships. Emotional awareness prevents them from understanding how their feelings impact their behaviour and interactions with others.

Identifying emotions and regulating them is gaining momentum; however, the majority still struggles with this because, from a young age, many are taught to either suppress emotions or discourage too much emotional expression. Over time, this leads to disconnection from one's emotional state, literally becoming numb and confused.

There is a societal tendency to downplay emotions and focus on logical and practical thinking, choosing to fill oneself up with external achievements in a way that inner experiences are silenced. We hide behind technology, perpetual scrolling, fast-paced lifestyles and distractions.

When individuals say "I don't know?", it can be the laziest, most convenient and helpless statement. Lack of emotional awareness leads to unresolved feelings. The emotions which are ignored, denied or suppressed don't simply disappear, but instead, they intensify over time. Those emotions find their own unique place in the body and show up as pain, aches, diseases, and sometimes, even cancer.

Science also proves this! Research by UCLA psychologist Mathew Lieberman found that simply identifying and labelling our emotions can significantly improve our emotional health. It activates the pre-frontal cortex areas in the brain, responsible for rational thinking and decision making, while reducing the activity in the amygdala, the brain's emotional centre. This prevents difficult emotions from escalating, making it easier to manage heavy emotions like stress, frustration, anger and doubt.

This brings us back to the raw, hard and negative emotions mentioned earlier. One can observe Robert Plutchik's 'Theory of Evolution of Emotions', and Dr Gloria Wilcox's expansion on the same theory. They are both significant tools to become aware of and understand one's emotions. According to Plutchik, the concept of emotions applies to all evolutionary levels and hence is present in plants, animals and humans. Emotions played an adaptive role in helping organisms address key survival challenges posed by the environment. Emotions have various layers, there are primary emotions that are pairs of opposites. Each emotion can exist in varying degrees of intensity. He identified eight primary emotions:

- Joy (Happiness)
- Trust (Admiration)
- Fear (Apprehension)
- Surprise (Amazement)
- Sadness (Grief)
- Disgust (Loathing)
- Anger (Rage)
- Anticipation (Interest)

Dr Gloria Wilcox expanded on Plutchik's work by developing her own version of the wheel of emotions, which branches into further nuanced emotions. This model can help individuals to articulate their feelings more precisely. Let us explore how emotions can be broken down into deep inner states and layers:

Anger- At the core, anger is an instinctual response to fight or defend against threats.

1. The milder versions of anger are annoyance, irritation and frustration. This could be because of some obstacles preventing progress of work, or triggered by inconveniences or personal boundaries are pushed continuously.
2. Resentment is when anger is suppressed or prolonged, typically felt in relationships where unresolved issues linger. This is the common cause behind certain diseases when this negativity

shows up as pains, inflammation, arthritis or even certain cancers, such as cancer of the breast in women.

3. Rage and fury are the most intense forms of anger, which show up as extreme violent behaviour. Hostility is the same version, except its build up over a longer period of time.
4. Anger can be a defence mechanism in the case of feelings of fear, hurt or shame. This is used to protect themselves from losing control or cover up their real feelings.

Understanding the layers of anger through Dr Wilcox's wheel enables individuals to understand and dissect their deeper emotional experiences. They can recognise whether they are merely frustrated because of annoying people or traffic before work, and more importantly, they would realise that it's not in their control. Furthermore, they could be feeling angry because of some bitterness, which could be decoded to some violation in the recent past, or maybe childhood. The aggression could be because of being provoked, about which they were unaware. The anger could also appear because they were let down, stemming from some betrayal. Just the awareness about our innermost emotions empowers us to work on the trigger and figure out a wiser response.

Fear- The emotion of fear emanates from a possible threat of known or unknown, triggering a fight or flight response, immediate or prolonged.

1. Milder forms of fear are apprehension associated with the uncertainty of the future. This shows up in the body, breath and thoughts as nervousness or unease.

2. Moderate forms of fear show up as anxiety or worry, a state of tension without a definite cause. This affects the mental and, subsequently the physical health. Doubt is also one such fear which impairs decision-making.
3. Intense forms of fear range from terror to panic to horror, causing deep-seated trauma. Here, the response of the body is completely different.
4. Being fearful could also emanate from certain deep emotional feelings which are not easy to detect. These could be feelings of weakness because of being treated as insignificant, being constantly excluded, and hence a looming feeling of rejection. Feeling of insecurity from an inferiority complex, or simply feeling weak and worthless.

Fear is just an outer face of something deep brewing inside, and knowing that deeper crux can be powerful.

Bad feeling- The most overused and under-understood feeling is 'Bad'. Going deeper, it reflects discomfort, heaviness, unease or moral wrongdoing. Being vague, it could mean anything, has a vast range, basically, something is not right either in the situation, with oneself or in response to others.

1. Milder forms of bad could mean feeling emotional or physical unease in a place, or with people slightly out of place. It could be boredom emanating from lack of interest, motivation, and engagement. It may also be stemming from empathy for others or unmet expectations, such that things are not the way they should be.
2. Moderate forms of bad could be unfocused, tired or rushed

3. Intense feeling of bad could have its root in feeling overwhelmed, hence confused, out of control because of stress.

It is very enlightening to go under the layers of 'Bad' because the only opposite one knows is good, and to make oneself good, there are cheap, short-term hacks such as overdose of cupcakes, alcohol or even drugs.

Disgust: This is another powerful emotion that we think protects us from things we perceive as harmful or repulsive, whether it be sight, smell, touch, situation or someone's behaviour.

1. Mild forms of disgust could include dislike, rejection, displeasure, or aversion
2. Moderate intensity of disgust could be disappointed or disapproving. When one goes deeper, it could be because of our own judgments, black or white mindset, or preconceived stereotypes.
3. Intense form of disgust is loathing emanating from hatred, maybe because of old traumas, incidents, or repetitive negative behaviour of others. It could also be rooted in moral outrage, unethical behaviour, or injustice.

The beauty about disgust is that it's a natural red flag your body is giving you to be rooted in your own values, identify toxic situations, distance oneself from potentially offensive people and situations, not provoked, identify your judgements and so on.

Sadness: One of the most depleting forms of emotions. At its core is a biting sense of hurt due to loss. This could be loss of a loved one, a missed opportunity, or unfulfilled desires. It is a natural response to the cyclical nature of life, its hardships and challenges.

1. Mild sadness is disappointment when expectations are not met, Discouragement when efforts don't yield results, or pity for someone. This degree of sadness is positive because it pushes us to do better, put in some more effort and find awareness.
2. A mild degree of sadness has roots in feeling vulnerable, powerless, and in despair. If sadness is at the surface, then deeper emotion could be loneliness, which again has further roots in either low self-confidence or a feeling of abandonment stemming from childhood.
3. Intense sadness arises from a pathetic feeling of guilt, again instilled in childhood. Guilt is the most negative and man-made emotion as it is related to societal norms, cultural conditioning and moral values that are learned rather than being an innate biological response.
4. Unlike basic emotions such as anger or fear, which are present from birth and serve evolutionary functions, guilt is instilled through upbringing as a measure of control, to make belief right or wrong or match societal expectations. This emotion leads to self-blame, locks one in shame and a feeling of inadequacy.

Grief due to loss could also lead to sadness at the surface.

Happiness: The most loved and positive polarity that reflects joy, contentment, and so on. It is an emotion that has a vast array of deeper feelings, such that just by being aware of these feelings, the brain and heart get filled with joy.

1. At the very essence, happiness is a light-headed feeling of being playful, cheeky, free. It could also be due to inquisitiveness or curiosity. Pure love and respect are happy feelings
2. Being happy could mean being courageous, proud, confident, powerful, creative, accepted, valued or successful.
3. At a deeper sense, it could be a feeling of ecstasy, euphoria or just peace and bliss.

Recognising the layers, tints of happiness change the physical, emotional, and mental state into different forms of positivity. Whether through finding simple pleasures in daily life, looking for blissful experiences or understanding deeper connections.

All emotions exist in polarity and intensity. Every emotion has its unique place because it serves a distinct function in helping navigate life, adapt to changes, increase awareness, and make decisions. Instead of 'Good' or 'Bad', emotions need to be unfurled to get valuable information about the internal state and relationship with the environment.

Fear helps to recognise fight or flight triggers, ensuring deeper work in self-preservation and building long-term resilience. Awareness about **anger** can help understand the underlying feeling and that it is a symptom of something bigger. The question to ask in the loom of **sadness**- where is it coming from? It is the effect, so what is the cause of this feeling?

Disgust helps to know the moral compass, draw boundaries and possibly stand up for something. Feelings of **joy** and **courage** give a glimpse of possibilities and human potential. They push the boundaries. **Trust**, **respect**, and **love** are bedrocks of collaboration, connections, and communities.

Human beings, at individual levels, are not capable of growth and development. They need motivation, drive or simple love. A study on "The Neuroscience of Growth Mindset and Intrinsic Motivation" that featured college students revealed that students given financial incentives to solve puzzles quit soon once payment stopped, whereas their intrinsically motivated peers kept improving their speed and strategy. The key for the latter candidates was their inner motivation.

Much like oil in a machine, emotions ensure smooth functioning of the human experience, reducing friction, wear and tear. As life is cyclical, there will be ups and downs, and the right emotions make us aware of this and help in adapting to changes. They help in distilling meaningful situations and finding the right path. Human life is not to be wasted and to be put to a higher good for evolution and growth; this understanding is facilitated by emotions.

Certain destructive emotions such as hate, guilt, remorse, repentance and shame, which may linger or be prolonged, have a paralysing effect on personal development, isolating relationships, slowing down growth, affecting finances, even cause chronic diseases since the body holds the feelings. An end-to-end meta-analysis of 112 studies (9,277 participants) found a large negative correlation between shame and self-esteem, and low self-esteem, in turn, predicted diminished motivation in individuals.

Remaining stuck for too long, the extreme polarities can cause prolonged physical and psychological diseases. Moving to the centre, finding a balance and regulating emotions enable individuals to bring clarity and not be consumed by the situation. It means to take responsibility for the emotions, not to suppress them; it's about acknowledging them, regulating them without letting them control our behaviour.

Arjun had carried an incredible amount of anger toward his father for years. His father's harsh criticism in childhood never made him feel "good enough." Even as an adult, resentment showed up- arguments at home, a short fuse with his own children and an inability to express warmth.

The tables dramatically turned when, one day, his own teenage daughter blurted out in frustration, "You never appreciate me, papa (dad). Just like dadu (grandpa) never appreciated you." The words pierced him. He realised he was unconsciously becoming the very person he resented.

That night, sitting alone, he asked himself: "Do I want to pass this anger to the next generation? Or, do I want to end it here?" Forgiveness became his answer- to release himself from the generational prison of resentment. Slowly, he softened toward his father and, more importantly, toward his children.

A relevant anecdote that depicts how forgiveness frees us from negative emotions is the case of generational resentment.

Opposites Don't Just Attract!

One of the most powerful emotions, and a superpower that can transmute extreme feelings, is Forgiveness. It is a bridge between two emotions standing at loggerheads, stuck in time. It helps in releasing the intensity of the emotion sitting at the fence. It involves acknowledging the negative emotion, such as anger, resentment, hatred, disgust towards oneself, a situation or another person. It is a conscious decision to work out these negative emotions before forgiving. This does not mean denying or suppressing negative emotions to look larger than life.

Gratitude, compassion, and forgiveness are not just complex emotions- they are superpowers. They are the hidden truths, secret formulae to happiness, a blend of math, physics and chemistry leading to the alchemy of transformation. Intense, raw, misunderstood emotions can be transformed into refined power, which can be used to propel one's growth. Like a skilled alchemist turning base metals into gold.

Gratitude has the power to turn the feeling of weakness, rejection, inadequacy, and even fear into pure joy, faith and optimism. It has the power to collapse the past and future into the present. It can take you to a zone which has no time and space, just pure joy.

Compassion is an alchemist that transmutes sadness, hurt, pain, disappointment into unconditional love, peace and trust.

It has the power to transcend limitations and create something never done before.

Forgiveness is the magic wand that can turn any negative, harmful or destructive emotion, such as resentment, hatred, anger, disgust, etc to pure joy, happiness, peace, contentment, courage and confidence. It is known that everything has its place and staying in the negative will only do self-harm.

The idea of forgiveness has many shades of real-world practicality. It acknowledges and understands the root cause of prolonged negative emotions, and works to regulate and release them, allowing us to forgive ourselves and others, is better than living with self-sabotage of emotional drainage and paralysis, impaired judgement, stagnation, and disconnection.

Looking at the situation from an objective perspective acts as a catalyst for emotional alchemy. When the focus is shifted from a personal, emotionally disorientated charged view to a more neutral and detached outlook, a psychological distance is created from the intensity of the feelings. Simply speaking, when we refrain from getting over-emotional about things and rather look at the broader picture, a healthy barrier is established between us and intense feelings.

To understand the broader picture, feelings have to be detached from the situation. This can be done by changing the question in the mind, from "Why is this happening to me" to "Yes, this has happened. What can I learn from this?", thus empowering one to move from reactive to proactive thinking.

Once the charge of the initial triggering incident is down, emotional alchemy begins. Essentially, the brain is being rewired not to get stuck in a loop of negative repetitive thinking. It breaks away and starts to create new neuro-pathways of constructive higher emotional state. An fMRI study found that just 4 days of brief mindfulness cut amygdala reactivity, while boosting prefrontal control circuits. This essentially means, in just 4 days of mindfulness practice, the brain's alarm centre calmed down, while the pre-frontal cortex became more active to promote better self-control.

The shift towards mindfulness requires courage as well as a willingness to change. It requires a little amount of work to ask uncomfortable questions, such as, "What have I been feeling and what is the underlying cause of my reaction", or "What am I missing here which I am not doing to feel this way.

Hermes Trismegistus, ancient philosopher associated with wisdom, alchemy and esoteric teachings, spoke about 'The Principle of Paradox', one of the seven principles in his book, 'The Kybalion'. It explains the idea of opposites fundamentally interconnected, forming a whole. Taking the concepts of heat and cold, the paradox claims that heat and cold are both temperatures; the distinction is their relative vibration rate. Temperature is a measure of the average kinetic energy, or the microscopic vibration rate of molecules in a substance. More energy means faster vibrations (we call this hot); less energy means slower vibrations (we call this cold). Move the thermometer and the labels switch gradually; there is no absolute line.

Similarly, Hermetic philosophy suggests that every emotion has two extremes or poles, yet these opposites are just different degrees of the same thing. For example, love and hate, hot and cold, light and dark or right or wrong. The essence of paradox is seemingly opposite forces that are connected and part of one big whole.

Paradoxically, opposites are the same in nature, yet differ in degree. For example, hot and cold are both forms of temperature, love and hate are forms of emotion. What we perceive as conflicting forces are from the same origin, just different in intensity. Once we know this aspect, we can master the art of transforming one into another.

According to Hermes Trismegistus, the solution to the polarity of paradoxes is not in choosing one side over the other, but rather by realising that both sides are important and complementary. True wisdom lies in accepting both ends and their interdependence. He speaks of unity of opposites- light and dark, above and below, spirit and matter. The idea here is of true oneness- that all things arise from the same source and are connected, and transformation is the process of harmonising opposites. Spiritual alchemists consider this to be the basis of transmutation of the true nature- the soul. Which means that if everything is from the same source, as it comes down into duality, it loses the original form, and by purification and transformation, it can return to its original state.

Every event has a corresponding effect on its material and energy state. Alchemy, in this sense, is a process of transforming one's inner self from a lower to a higher vibration or state of consciousness. Imagine what state of consciousness are the emotions of anger and joy. This is what Buddha propagated, turning the physical 'Lead' of desires, ignorance, and limiting beliefs into 'Gold' of wisdom, purity and awareness of all forms to make informed choices. To understand the process of spiritual alchemy, we need to understand six layers:

1. The inward voyage

Gnosis- the first step in spiritual alchemy is an ancient Hermetic axiom, "Know thyself". To begin to transform your vibrations, you need to know who you are at the core, what works for you and what gets the darker side out. This will help you to identify the areas in your life where you operate from lower vibrations, such as intense desires, attachment, anger, etc. These are emotional weights or baggage that keep you anchored in the lower vibrations.

Reflect on the hurt, resentment, grudge you carry and the guilt or shame trip you go on to. Notice how it affects your feelings, mood, relationships and even any association of the same with physical body issues. Avoidance solidifies the pain.

2. Rise from the ashes

In alchemy, purification(calcination) is a process required to burn away. The purification is a very important step in transforming any material. This process removes impurities and unwanted substances from substances to enhance their physical and chemical properties increasing the purity, strength, resistance to corrosion, and conductivity.

Similarly, this process is essential for human existence and active transformation. Purification enables one to access the inner superpowers which are deep within, weighed down by the baggage of heavy judgments, conditioning, and emotions which cloud the mind. It starts with keeping the physical body healthy through healthy food exercises.

Fasting during major festivals across cultures has its roots in purification. It cleanses the body, clears the mind, and develops willpower. From the aspect of emotional purification, releasing repressed emotions, resolving past traumas enable healthier emotional responses.

Psychologically, not going back to the same thoughts and limiting beliefs, but rather creating new positive thought patterns, helps clear the mind, take better, quicker decisions. It leads to the process of 'Detachment', 'Letting go' and moving from lower vibrations by regulating emotional obstacles such as anger, pride, hate, etc. At another level, it means letting go of the need to hold on to the identity of being wronged. Often, holding a grudge serves the shadow self as it provides a hold, righteousness, and a reason for certain actions.

Cultural rituals, traditions and practices are hidden forms of purification and use elements of nature in the process. Water is a universal symbol of purification. Sacred rivers, holy water, are used to signify purification and rebirth. The River Nile's flooding was one such symbology. Rituals such as washing feet before prayers in Islam or Hindu temples, the Christian practice of baptism, having water from Holy places, and so on are proof of a similar thought process. Earth, as an element, is used in building places of worship which are highly charged with spiritual energy. Materials such as ashes, clay and sand are also used to cleanse the energy field. Fire is an element used to burn away impurities. This element has been worshipped and used as a tool in fire ceremonies in cultures such as Hindu's Havan or Hoil, Parsi Fire Temples, candles in churches, etc. Air is seen as the element of mind, used through burning of incense such as sandalwood, frankincense, sage and so on. Cleansing the body and mind through breathwork, pranayama in yoga, is a form of purification.

3. The metamorphosis

This stage, involving dissolution and separation (Transmutation), is a process of turning negative into positive, whether that be emotions, traits, or habits. It is a conscious effort to move from fear to faith, sadness to joy, despair to hope, a mindset of lack to abundance, resentment to forgiveness, compassion, and gratitude. By choosing to always be in higher vibrations, and no longer let the negative control or define you.

4. Joining hands

Conjunction (Integration) is the stage to integrate all aspects of learning and put it in practice. In alchemy, after the transformation of the substance, there is a process of integration where a new element is accepted and integrated into the whole. The lessons from life's experiences need to be rolled out for new habits to be developed.

The higher knowledge cannot be kept in ideas or ideals; it must be put into practice in today='s action. With so much knowledge flowing freely, the next big challenge for humanity is to be able to put it to good use. This step is akin to yoga- not just the asanas- rather a union of the lower nature with the higher. The higher nature automatically takes over the mind and emotions. Another perspective is that one no longer works from the sympathetic nervous system.

When we change, forgive, and learn, we move forward with wisdom. The process is complete when we can look back on the event or the person without being triggered by seeing it as a lesson in personal growth.

5. Evolution

At the fermentation (illumination) stage, you start to experience life from an elevated state. There is intention and a higher purpose behind every spoken word and action taken. There is heightened awareness and continuous deep inner work. This does not mean to renounce the world of desires, but rather to use desires to understand deeper levels of truth.

6. A new life

The final stage of Distillation (Living in harmony with the divine) is the state where gratitude, love, compassion, oneness and forgiveness are a way of being. These become instinctive in nature. This does not mean challenges will reduce; on the contrary they will transform into opportunities to practice the inner aligned state. This is the state when one starts to focus on service, giving what is received to continue the upward spiral of evolution.

The concept of a chain in discipleship applies here; the chain must move on for the wheel to move forward. A hook in the chain draws inspiration from someone who is a step ahead and pulls the one up who is behind. This is the way humanity will move forward.

The Perfect Frequency

Let's unbox the concept of Seven Rays from esoteric teachings and the works of Alice Bailey. Alice A. Bailey expanded an array of theosophical hints into a detailed science of "the seven rays." She saw these seven beams of cosmic energy as building-blocks of consciousness. The Seven Rays are believed to be cosmic principles representing different archetypes of energies and vibrations, much like a prism breaking the white light into seven colours with individual, unique qualities and attributes.

These teachings suggest that each person has a dominant personality and, hence a dominant ray type. Humanity is evolving through these ray types to higher vibrations. Recognising which ray type dominates your life can help you strengthen the core personality as well as areas of growth and potential weaknesses that come with that ray. For the world to exist, all the rays are necessary, and each person has to imbibe some parts of other rays as well.

In business and relationships, this information is valuable to understand where the other person comes from and how to harmonise various personalities. Each ray has its lower and higher vibrations; understanding and forgiveness are tools for transmuting the lower qualities into higher ones.

Once we understand ourselves better, we will become aware of our shadow self- everything that we deny about ourselves, hide or don't want to face or acknowledge, because these are parts of us which we have disowned. These are buried parts which still influence our behaviour. Each ray carries its distinct energy that guides how we approach situations. Dissecting into each ray, we get:

First Ray- The Ray of Will

Qualities: Leadership, Strength, Will, Power

Purpose: The energy of initiation, determination and purpose

Core: This ray represents the force of pure will. It is the energy that makes things happen, brings change, inspires leadership and action. It carries the ability to make decisive decisions and take charge. Driving forward innovation and transformation motivates them. Breaks through obstacles through sheer force

Challenges: Tendency towards domination, impatience and aggressiveness.

Shadow Aspects:

- Dominance- Desire to control or overpower

- Aggression- Excessive willpower can turn into aggressive behaviour, rigidity and inability to compromise
- Isolation- Because they cannot control everything, they become too self-reliant, shutting themselves off emotionally

Shadow Work:

- Learn to develop a balance between power and compassion for self and others.
- Forgive and let go of mistakes.
- Release rigidity, create space for genuine, mutual connections.

Personalities- Winston Churchill, Steve Jobs

Second Ray- The Ray of Love

Qualities: Love, Compassion, Understanding

Purpose: Heal, Connect, Nurture

Core: This ray is associated with nurturing, teaching, healing, and mentorship. People with Ray Two energy have a deep understanding, empathy and a desire to connect and help people. It is an energy of binding through love and wisdom.

Challenges: Over-sensitivity, attachment, emotional dependence

Shadow Aspects:

- Over Giving- Sacrificing too much, leading to burnout or resentment
- Over Attachment- An overdeveloped need to help people turns into unhealthy overdependence

- Martyrdom- A limiting belief that individuals need to suffer for the sake of others to give and receive love, leading to overextension and self-neglect

Shadow Work:

- Release attachments to past hurts, traumas and grudges.
- Balance love and intelligence. Learn to love others without losing oneself. Create healthy boundaries.
- Emotionally detach from the outcome. Practice self-compassion.
- Recognise that helping others means enabling them to do what they are supposed to, not making them dependent.

Personalities: Mahatma Gandhi, Dalai Lama

Third Ray- The Ray of Active Intelligence

Quality: Adaptability, Intelligence, Flexibility

Purpose: Flow, disperse knowledge, Solve Problems, use intelligence to create solutions

Core: This ray is behind data, knowledge, learning, problem-solving, and ideas. People who resonate with this ray tend to be analytical, adaptable, and quick thinkers.

Challenges: Mental overactivity, restlessness, manipulation

Shadow Aspects:

- Manipulation- Using intelligence to outsmart or deceive others.
- Restlessness- A constant need for activity, instability and lack of focus

- Over-rationalisation- Overthink, overanalyse and overintellectualise, detaching from intuition or discernment.

Shadow work:

- Release mental judgements, excessive criticism, and the need to always be 'right.'
- Be intellectually humble by accepting that mistakes and miscommunication are part of life's learning process.
- Ray three needs to cultivate emotional intelligence, compassion and intuition.
- They must learn to practice gratitude for their mental gifts and use them for the greater good rather than just personal gains.

Personalities: Albert Einstein, Bill Gates, Jeff Bezos, Leonardo Di Vinci

Fourth Ray- The Ray of Harmony

Qualities: Harmony, Beauty, Creativity

Purpose: Restore balance of opposites, create harmony and conflict resolution, and diplomacy

Core: This ray is all about finding beauty in chaos, harmonising other rays, uniting opposite poles, promoting balance and artistic expression.

Challenges: Prone to conflict, Inner tension, Emotional Instability

Shadow aspects:

- Over-Sensitivity- Tendency to take things personally

- Avoidance of conflict- Some Ray 4 may avoid confrontation, creating inner turmoil instead of addressing the root cause
- Drama and Chaos- When unbalanced, this ray can over exaggerate, or create conflict as a means to express suppressed emotions.

Shadow work:

- Forgiving people and accepting both sides of the situation to arrive at a win-win outcome
- Integrating lessons
- Creating a higher synthesis

Personalities: John Lennon, Nelson Mandela, Pablo Picasso, Mark Zuckerberg

Fifth Ray- The Ray of knowledge with data, science

Qualities: Knowledge, Science, Logic, Precision

Purpose: Pursue Inquiry knowledge and scientific methods

Core: This ray embodies objective knowledge. It encourages investigation, research, truth through logic and hard facts. Doctors, Scientists, Researchers, Engineers, etc embody this ray type.

Challenges: Rigidity, Scepticism, Unhealthy detachment

Shadow aspect:

- Coldness or detachment- Manifests as emotional detachment or valuing facts over feelings

- Dogmatism- A rigid attachment to logic and facts leads to close-mindedness, stopping the flow of intuition and openness to other perspectives.
- Criticism- Ray 5 may become overly critical of themselves and others, chasing perfectionism and losing compassion.

Shadow work:

- Letting go of the need for absolute proof.
- It is about developing faith and accepting that not everything can be analysed or understood logically.
- Create room for free flow, creativity, and chance. Ingrate empathy with practicality.

Personalities: Madame Curie, Newton, Rosalind Franklin

Sixth Ray- The Ray of Devotion

Quality: Devotion, Faith, Sacrifice, Idealism

Purpose: Service, Spread devotion and faith

Core: This ray commits itself to service to a higher cause, devotion to a purpose such that they are willing to make any sacrifices for that.

Challenges: Fanaticism, Dogmatism, Emotional Idealism

Shadow aspects:

- Fanaticism- Blind devotion to a cause leading to intolerance or extremism
- Emotional over exaggeration- May become overly passionate when their beliefs are challenged.

- Attachment to ideals- Overattachment to visions can make them delusional

Shadow work:

- Driven by strong ideals, these people must work on letting go of unrealistic expectations of others and themselves.
- Need to develop gratitude and compassion when ideals are not met.
- Need to develop tolerance to be developed to appreciate different viewpoints.

Personalities: Mother Teresa, Malala Yousafzai

Seventh Ray- The Ray of Order

Quality: Order, Organisation, Ritual, Ceremonies

Purpose: Transformation through bringing order

Core: People of this ray work with systems towards order and structure. They bring ideas into reality through rituals and action.

Challenges: Rigidity, Over-emphasis on rules, Mechanical repetition

Shadow Aspect:

- Rigidity- The lower aspect of Ray 7 manifests as inflexibility or becoming too attached to rules, routines, and traditions
- Over attachment to form- This Ray may focus too much on material or outer form, losing sight of the purpose behind the form.

- Perfectionism- This may create frustration when expectations are not met, or when things do not go as per the plan or when things go out of control

Shadow work:

- Rigid structure and rules can be stagnating or confining; they must be transformed into adaptability and acceptance.
- It is about understanding that rituals and order are tools for growth, not ends in themselves.
- This is the reason behind the death of cultures, religions and rituals.
- Self-imposed restrictions and limited beliefs must be given up.

Personalities: Nikola Tesla, J.K. Rowling

There is a symbiotic relationship between the higher rays and their lower correspondent rays. This connection goes with the hermetic principle of 'As above so below. As within so without.

This further explains the duality of things- every concept has a higher purpose and its functionality, which vibrates at the lowest level of practicality. This allows the higher qualities to be implemented in the day-to-day.

Ray 1 embodies the qualities of leadership, courage, strength and dynamism, while **Ray 7** represents organisation, structure, standard operating principles, thus manifesting the higher principles into practice.

Ray 2 focuses on love, compassion, empathy and understanding, while **Ray 6** emphasises devotion, service, and commitment. Love sees itself manifesting through serving others, internal motivation towards an ideal and forgiveness.

Ray 3 is adaptability, creativity, and abstract thinking, whereas **Ray 5** is all about intellectual ability, analytical thinking, and data. This is appropriate for technology products where design meets programming, or organisations where ideas meet strategy and viability.

The primary ray governing any person represents the core aspect of the identity, shaping the behaviour and the life path. The secret to harnessing the knowledge of one's ray is to integrate qualities from the higher or the lower correspondence of the ray and other rays as well. The evolution will happen when all the rays merge into one, creating an ideal human, like white light. The full potential of every human lies in these 7 rays. By identifying the underdeveloped areas and work on them strategically is the aim to develop the superpower.

The world needs more harmonisers, leaders with compassion, creativity with collaboration and knowledge with faith and devotion. The world does not need authoritative leaders to bring change; it needs collaborations, empowerment, communities, and empathetic connections. This world will be taken forward by individuals who know the secret that power lies in harmony, unity and valuing uniqueness and diversity.

Understanding the seven rays as guiding principles of our thinking, behaviour and habits gives a better and clearer grasp of what's going on. One's natural strengths can be embraced and enhanced since each ray carries distinct qualities of will to push through, love and compassion or active intelligence. This aligns with the higher purpose, and one doesn't need to struggle to succeed.

This gives us the intelligence to realise that others act according to their own unique energy blueprint, for example, in a group Ray 1 will come with force, while Ray 2 will come with softness and Ray 3 will talk facts and Ray 4 will know that all are right and will try to harmonise. This knowledge makes forgiveness an empowered choice rather than a forced reaction.

A simple yet unforgettable instance of internal forgiveness? Manish, a corporate professional, had been betrayed by a close friend who stole his business idea. The wound stayed with him. Over the years, he lost his spark. He found it hard to trust people, snapped at colleagues, and carried a quiet anger that weighed him down. Eventually, it showed in his health too- rising blood pressure and sleepless nights.

The turning point came unexpectedly. In a team meeting, a colleague complained that Manish never gave credit for others' contributions. The words hit him hard. On his way home that evening, he kept asking himself: What am I doing all this for? What has this anger really given me? That moment of self-honesty made him see the truth- he wasn't punishing the friend who betrayed him. He was punishing himself for not acting on his idea. Forgiveness, he realised, was not about the friend at all. It was about cutting the chain that kept him tied to bitterness.

As he began to let go- slowly, awkwardly at first- something shifted. The heaviness lifted, his health improved, and most importantly, his creativity returned. New ideas flowed again. Forgiveness became his doorway back to life.

Finding Inner Strength

The word 'Forgive' comes from the Old English 'Forgief', broken down into two words: For- Suggests 'To', 'In Advance' or 'Completely', and Giefan means 'To Give'.

Thus, 'Forgive' originally carries the idea of letting go of something entirely, particularly the notion of resentment, claim to retribution, revenge, grievance, etc. It is a process of release, letting go to give love, peace, and acceptance a chance.

Think about the energy, vibration or frequency of betrayal, hurt, neglect, mistreatment, abuse, jealousy, competition, failure, and so on. Hoarding negative, heavy barb like, heaty, smoky, dark, and stale emotions eats up the body from inside. Now compare these with the vibration of love, peace, courage, strength, joy, etc. These energies regenerate, renew, and heal the body.

Forgiveness opens up a space of power, where there is a conscious choice to respond without letting the past destroy the present and the future. This is the super which creates new realities coming from wisdom.

Wisdom is a combination of knowledge and love. Knowledge is heightened awareness that you can free yourself from the past judgements and controls, and that there is a far higher possibility beyond. Love is the infinite energy which goes beyond the time and space of the current reality.

When forgiveness comes from a space of wisdom and an intention of triggering the inner superpower, it creates an energy of immense love for oneself, others, the space around, without losing oneself. While forgiveness is a higher power, it must be rooted in respect to be truly grounded. Respect ensures self-identity and boundaries.

When you forgive, there is a release of tension, stress and other emotional burdens carried by the body, causing fresh energy of determination, confidence and joy to hold space. It can realign bonds that were broken, it can bring people closer than ever before, and it helps us let go and start afresh from zero.

In life, it's an unfortunate truth that many families, especially siblings, sometimes grow apart due to squabbles ranging from small misunderstandings to bigger issues. Forgiveness could be the first balm to heal such wounds.

Rita hadn't spoken to her brother in five years after a bitter inheritance dispute. Every festival felt incomplete, every family gathering uncomfortable. Deep down, she missed the old bond; hurt and pride held her back.

Life gave the siblings a second chance when their mother fell ill. The mother gathered them both and, with tears in her eyes, said softly, "Don't fight anymore. One day your children may do the same to you — and you will feel helpless". Those words cut through the wall of silence. For the first time, Rita saw beyond the property, beyond the anger — into the future, she didn't want to pass on the same pattern to her children or live with guilt.

She reached out first, whispering, "Let us leave the past behind and go back to being buddies". Her brother broke down in tears. The ice melted, even though the property issue wasn't magically solved. They began talking again, sharing responsibilities for their mother.

A study published in the Annals of Behavioural Medicine, analysed a diverse community sample and found that week-to-week increases in state of forgiveness were followed by decreases in perceived stress, which in turn led to improvements in mental health symptoms, supporting a "forgiveness leads to less stress leads better health pathway".

When you internally forgive, the release of weight is so powerful that in most cases, the external action of confrontation, demanding an apology, asking for forgiveness, or direct face-to-face resolution is no longer necessary. You do not need to 'fix' the situation. Your newfound control over the negative emotion gives you a release, whereby the negative situation or the trigger no longer exists. The reason being, forgiveness isn't about them, it's about you!

The sign that forgiveness is done is when the same event, situation, person or behaviour no longer triggers discomfort or an unwanted response. There is a mental resolution and a feeling of peace. In many cases, the trigger or the memory of the situation no longer exists. One can meet the same person without any baggage.

Let's hark back to the hermetic principle in the Kybalion, which mentions "The Law of Correspondence- As above; so below. As within; so without". This principle suggests that most patterns, situations and relationships mirror what is going on inside us. The microcosm (Our thoughts, emotions, behaviour, habits, spoken words, etc) is reflected in the macrocosm (The space, situations, others' behaviour towards us, the universe at large). We need to align the inner self to change the outer world.

Forgiveness does not prevent accountability, or not standing up for your values, or not taking rightful action, or letting people in your safe space. Wisdom states that knowledge of wrongdoing has come into your space to show you how to better the situation. Hence, when an action is taken for justice, it should be done after the process of forgiveness so that the intention is not to get square, or punish or feel guilty or take revenge.

The appropriate action is defined by an intention of compassion, such that we are humans, we will make mistakes, it's part of our journey and evolution. These mistakes are rooted in one's own struggles, ignorance, misplaced ego, a very narrow upbringing of the mind, deprivation of love and justice, and long existence with fear and pain.

The Torah, the sacred texts of Judaism, blends divine forgiveness with human forgiveness as responsibility, compassion, and personal growth. There are thirteen attributes of mercy. It is seen as an essential value for personal, communal, and national harmony. The concept of 'Shalom' or peace is the anchor. The Torah also acknowledges that forgiveness can be difficult, particularly for serious wrongs, and some harms which are serious or repetitive require justice.

As a hypnotherapist, I was working with a woman who struggled to connect with her own needs, prioritising her husband, children, parents, and parent in laws above herself. She felt guilty doing basic, small things for herself. During one of our sessions, the therapy took an unexpected turn when an energy linked to the ancient practice of 'Sati', where women were burnt on the pyre of their husbands, emerged, influencing her because the client had been taken to a Sati temple right after her marriage. She had felt uncomfortable lighting the lamp because she was fundamentally against the principle of the 'Sati' practice. That is when the energy of the Sati started influencing her and guiding her inner voice.

The energy of Sati, through the client as a channel, revealed that she was burnt alive after her husband had passed away, much against her will, despite her desire to live, study and lead a purposeful life in guiding other women. She communicated that the ancestors of her in-laws and the local community had participated in the practice of Sati, leaving a lingering wound in the energy of the area and its collective consciousness. The environment had become patriarchal, leading to women being silenced, mistreated, emotionally unfulfilled and disrespected.

Interestingly, my client was a very confident person, being someone who broke the glass ceiling; however, after the marriage, she began experiencing disrespect in very subtle ways. She did not recognise the signs because tolerance, adjustments, and being silent are all virtues glorified to make sure women don't rebel.

In time, she started to recognise that family feuds over land are the collective ancestral negative karma. The lineage of disrespect continues, as they are required to be polite, soft spoken, and instilled with fear if they speak their mind or don't listen to authority. Power is held by the elders, even if they abuse authority- emotionally, by manipulation or with control. The gaslighting is that women show love by serving hot meals at any given time, sacrificing their needs to show affection, and solely taking care of the house, even if they are working. If they speak their mind, they are aggressive or manipulative.

My client began to comprehend the shift within, as she started to express her discomfort. She felt shut down and isolated. The sessions later uncovered fear instilled in women due to historical persecution of women, taking away authority and power from them across the world, making them weak and dependent. She was guided to cultivate courage and faith with the realisation that when one woman stands up for herself and makes a change, she breaks the cycle, impacting not just her generation, but also those yet to come.

In subsequent therapy sessions, she asked for forgiveness from the sati energy, being the bridge between the ancestors and all those women who were burnt. She was reminded to continue advocating against injustices and work with courage and confidence.

Sati in India, witch-burning in Europe and the Americas, the holocaust, persecution of identities, and so on, can still be witnessed in the modern form of discrimination, violence, objectification, generational traumas, collective memory of judgements, internalised shame, fear of expression, a sense of preserving the community to protect identity, and many more.

Forgiveness is not about forgetting the injustices; it rather serves as a powerful tool for personal liberation. This is moving beyond victimhood and rising towards empowerment. Once women heal and forgive, they can create safe spaces, build alliances and advocate for many to follow.

I vividly remember another one of my clients, a woman burdened by the stress of her husband's alcoholism and the pain of enduring years of physical, emotional, and mental trauma. She got diagnosed with cancer, which was the breaking point that made her take action and move out. Despite leaving her husband and removing herself from the toxic environment, she continued to be consumed by anger, hurt and deep resentment towards her husband.

Those unresolved emotions worsened her condition. She was then introduced to the concept of letting go through forgiveness and "The Twin Hearts Meditation" to bless. Initially, it seemed impossible to forgive someone who had caused her so much suffering, but, as she began her journey, something extraordinary happened.

Forgiveness did not mean to excuse her husband's addiction or invalidate his pain. She realised, as she practised every day, that it was a process of freeing herself from the entanglement and emotional chains that had kept her bound to the situation and the person. The continued resentment she was holding on to was harming her body rather than punishing or changing her husband.

The forgiveness process gradually released the anger and hurt which she had stored in her body, which had started to destroy her cells. She took a step further by blessing him in her meditation, which gave her tremendous peace. In time, her health improved dramatically, and she was inspired to teach others this powerful technique.

> *"Father, forgive them, for they don't know what they are doing"*
>
> **– Luke 23:24, The Bible**

Jesus was crucified, and despite the immense physical pain, there was no feeling of hurt for those who betrayed him. From a higher state of consciousness, he knew that they were ignorant, bound by judgments, old dogmatic ideas, and conditioning. From a space of infinite oneness, love and compassion, he asked for forgiveness for them.

This was Jesus's final test for resurrection. Forgiveness is the crucial catalyst that causes the death of the ego and connects to the unlimited superpowers within, which lead us to a rebirth of sorts. Forgiveness is the gateway to superpowers, through the death of the old self. The ego craves to keep us small, fragile, insignificant, and powerless. The mastery over the lower and self-limitations gradually opens the path to limitless miracles.

"There are only two ways to live your life. One is as though nothing is a miracle. The other is as though everything is a miracle."

– Albert Einstein

I once worked with a woman who had slipped into a coma after suffering a brain stroke. She was found in her room in the morning. Her husband, who had seen me helping her with a previous physical issue, reached out for healing. I connected with her consciousness or the soul, as her body was in a coma- a state of giving up hope, playing dead, lost. When I reached out to her, she revealed that the emotional neglect had led her to overthink. She could not communicate or express to anyone. Her husband was never around. She felt lost, disconnected and unseen.

I told her that every human at any point in time has a choice- she had a choice to remain in the lost state, which would mean continuing to be in a coma, suffering for both herself and her daughter. Or she could make a different choice- she could choose to forgive. I explained to her that her husband, though he had caused her emotional pain, was concerned and by her side, making an effort to take care of her in ways he hadn't before. Or she could leave the body, leaving her daughters to suffer even more for no fault.

I then spoke to her husband, urging him to connect with her in a way he had not before. At first, he was hesitant- "How can I talk to her, she is in a coma". I reassured him that while she couldn't respond physically, her soul, which is omnipresent and vibrates, has a higher consciousness to hear him. I encouraged him to talk to her, to let her know that he loves her and will do anything to take care of her. As he started doing that, through distant healing techniques of pranic healing, I could sense some shift in her energy.

After three days, I received a message from her husband. While he was talking to her, a few tears rolled down her cheeks. That was the sign, I asked him to get the daughters to talk to her, telling her she was wanted, loved and that they needed her to come back. She chose to return to her body, and even though partially paralysed, her husband is around her all the time, taking care of every small need.

Forgiveness begins with oneself, forgiving ourselves. It's about addressing the fragmented parts of our being which are left behind at various stages of life, when we are wounded by fears, traumas or situations carrying unresolved emotions. These parts, also referred to as 'Inner Child' carry the weight of the moments when we didn't know better, when we were made to feel guilty, unheard, unseen, or invalidated. They hold on to the heaviness of not being acknowledged, understood, and until we forgive and let go of these parts, we remain disconnected with our wholeness. Similar patterns keep repeating; the setting may be different.

These forgotten fragments show up as energy blocks, limitations, things we avoid, and we resist. They act as barriers, preventing us from fully embracing the wholeness and the greatness we are meant to embody. They are asking for our attention, waiting for us to address them first before we can move forward.

When we forgive ourselves, we acknowledge these wounded parts and release them, allowing light to shine in those dark alleys leading us to our authentic being. Forgiveness is a process which is ongoing, giving us our power back, making us recognise our worth, making us infinite, such that we are capable of rising above past experiences.

A woman's daughter once reached out to me for healing because her mother was battling cancer. Psychosomatically, cancer is linked to hoarding negative emotions such as resentment, anger and hatred towards oneself and others. Cancer does not happen in a day; years of giving room to the negative feelings in the cells of the body rot the whole basket.

When I was counselling the mother, I discovered she was a perfectionist, putting a lot of pressure on herself, quick to judge and harboured resentment towards certain family members. There was also an attachment to certain kinds of foods not as nourishment but as an emotional crutch. The body has an innate ability to heal itself, which is what I have experienced in pranic healing miracles.

As I worked with her, due to the pain and suffering, she was willing to practice forgiveness and the Twin Hearts Meditation. Medical treatment, cancer-specific nutrition and frequent healing sessions gave her much relief, and she made remarkable progress. Eventually, she was treated for cancer, and her results came out clear.

However, many months later, I received a call from my daughter again. The cancer had returned, and they were seeking healing once more. She had fallen back into her old habitual pattern, blaming people, becoming critical once again, not refraining from unhealthy eating. Negative emotional weight took over, and this time her body could not fight back. She passed away.

The brain has an incredible ability to create holographic images, which are commonly seen as vivid and often surreal experiences while we are dreaming. Dreams are projections of our internal world, like a movie playing in our minds that is non-linear, fragmented, and full of sensory perceptions and emotions. This is because the plane on which this is occurring is known as the astral world, hence the common mystical word-astral projection. Beyond the physical world that we see, there is no time and space. That is why we see dreams which are not connected, we see random people, at various times and different locations.

The brain does not store information in isolated drawers, rather in a network of patterns, bits, and pieces of experiences that are drawn upon and reassembled to create a whole image. Hence, you have the power to be innovative and creative to create an entirely new and dynamic image. This wave-like process allows the brain to access different parts of emotions, sensory data, thoughts, and memories simultaneously. This is why certain memories, fears, and traumas feel intensely real when triggered.

This process is the secret behind visualisation to manifest, a practice used by sportsmen, athletes, scientists, and innovators. When athletes such as Michael Phelps, Virat Kohli, Cristiano Ronaldo, etc visualise themselves playing the sport, swimming at a speed, hitting the ball with the bat to make a century or the football into the goal, they are training the brain to create a holographic reality of success. The brain rehearses not only the physical action, but also the emotional highs with equal intensity, embedding this experience in the subconscious. Scientists such as Albert Einstein and Nikola Tesla would recall visualising complex inventions or theories in their minds before bringing them to reality.

The fascinating thing about the brain is that it doesn't know what is real and what is imagined; both are created using the same neural pathways. The brain is just like a computer; thoughts, ideas, limitations, self-made rules, dreams, etc. are software programs. Whether the event is experienced in the physical world or intentionally, vividly imagined, the brain uses the same neural pathways, and if this is rehearsed many times over, the connection becomes strong.

We can consciously stop replaying old hurts, fears, and strategically erase all these, along with limiting beliefs and create new possibilities from the potential that can be tapped. Over time, new images are settled into the brain, and the old traumas or memories are forgotten, in the sense that the association of the emotional negative charge no longer exists.

True power lies in letting go, not in holding on to the past. Creating a false sense of control is such a lie and self-debilitating mindset. Choosing stagnation and halting personal growth over the ability to access personal power is the way to shut the doors to power, success, abundance, and love.

The ancient Egyptians believed that the heart, rather than the brain, was the centre of a person's intellect, emotions, and morality. It carried the repository of one's thoughts, deeds, and character during life. It is believed that 'The weighing of the heart' ceremony would take place where Anubis, God of the dead, would guide the deceased to the Hall of Ma'at, Goddess of truth, justice, harmony, and divine order. The heart of the deceased was placed on the set of scales and balanced against the feather of Maat.

A balanced, light heart would mean it did not carry any baggage; hence, the soul was sent to a heavenly place called 'The Field of Reeds. If the heart was heavier than the feather representing justice, harmony and truth, the heart would be devoured by Ammit, a fearsome creature. There was a lot of importance given to the virtues, moral conduct, harmony and that one's actions carried consequences even after death.

This ancient Egyptian belief that one's thoughts, behaviour, habits, and words would be the weight to decide the kind of afterlife the soul will lead is not unique to them. Various cultures, philosophical beliefs, and Near-Death Experiences (NDEs) propose the same concept. The parallels in 'The Law of Karma' in Hinduism and Buddhism, which is the law of cause and effect, where the soul must learn the lessons. The Christian idea of the final judgement, where one's life is evaluated on deeds and faith.

These shared motifs suggest that across cultures there is importance given to introspection, self-accountability, responsibility, consequences of actions and self- reflection.

Death & Forgiveness

The pre-death period is vividly described by many who went through Near-Death Experiences (NDE), which are powerful, transformative events when someone is very close to death, and has been medically dead for a brief period. NDEs shared by many provide insights into the process of death- there is a life review, encounters with spiritual beings, overwhelming compassion, forgiveness, love, and peace. Expanded consciousness, oneness with all and interconnectedness with the universe.

A 2001 prospective study of 344 cardiac-arrest survivors conducted by The Lancet found that 18% reported NDEs were characterised by elements such as profound peace, out-of-body perception, and encounters with light or beings. A long-term follow-up showed enduring transformations in values, as well as reduced fear of death.

Danion Brinkley, the author of 'Saved by the Light', was sent back with a mission to spread a message on awakening and preparing humanity for future changes. An American author and speaker best known for accounts of multiple near-death experiences (NDEs), he has described being struck by lightning and undergoing a panoramic life review, as well as encounters with "beings of light," and later having additional NDEs related to surgeries. Brinkley was sent back because his work on earth was not yet over; he had to work in helping others in the process of dying. He had to do service during the transition of the mindset to a more spiritually conscious world.

Anita Moorjani, diagnosed with terminal cancer, experienced a remarkable journey, documented by her doctors, in the book 'Dying to be me.' She was told by the beings that her cancer was rooted in deep fear, and the cure for illness was unconditional love for herself. Her purpose in returning to earth was to spread the message that with forgiveness and self-love and removal of fear, even cancer can be cured.

Dr Eben Alexander, a neurosurgeon, also had a near-death experience when he contracted a severe case of bacterial meningitis, which left him in a coma for a week. His medical background made him sceptical of what he was shown. "Proof of Heaven', his book, is a bestseller with a scientific perspective on NDEs, where he describes travelling through a dark realm referred to as the 'The Void'. After enduring that, he encounters his spiritual guide, and his mission upon returning was to talk about the consciousness that exists beyond the brain. He was given the responsibility to bridge the gap between science and spirituality. He was meant to share his experience to encourage people to rethink their actions, the nature of consciousness and question rigid materialist views.

Many other people have had NDEs, and the messages from all have the same themes:

- The core purpose of life is to operate from unconditional love and oneness.

- What you do to others is what you do to yourself, and the other way around as well.
- Service to others by showing compassion, guiding them through the spiritual journey.
- Before dying, one must leave negative thoughts behind, forgive and love.
- Healing and transformation can be hastened with self-love and forgiveness.
- Expand the awareness and spiritually awaken to find one's purpose
- Death is a process and should be honoured.

The process of dying, death and post-death is described in detail in many texts such as the Garuda Purana, The Tibetan Book of the Dead, Astara, Egyptian culture and many others. If we break it down, the common understanding is:

- Death is viewed as a temporary state of transition to liberation from certain purposes or lessons. It is not an end in itself.
- The soul is prepared before the actual time arrives to leave the body. One goes through a life review where the entire life is shown as a holographic movie. It is more vivid than when they were alive.
- The events are witnessed not just from their perspective, but from everyone's view who is involved. This creates a sense of empathy and awakening as to how their actions affected others.
- There is a guiding presence of a compassionate being, a spiritual guide, a spiritual teacher or even a deceased one. Life review is a learning process and not a punishment, hence the guide or the guides encourage reflection on the choices made.

- These guides are most compassionate, and it is described that humans judge themselves more and don't forgive themselves while reliving the moments of failure and unkindness.

Certain regrets people experience before nearing the end of their life are:

- **Not living true to themselves**:
  - Many realise that they spent too much time trying to meet the standards and expectations of society or the family instead of pursuing what truly made them authentic and happy.
- **Working too much:**
  - The regret is about spending too much time working instead of prioritising time with loved ones, rest and doing activities to spiritually evolve.
- **Not expressing feelings**
  - A common regret is not being open enough and acknowledging their feelings to their loved ones. Whether not saying 'I love you', not resolving conflicts, keeping emotions bottled up, or not forgiving. Many feel they missed the opportunity to be vulnerable and emotionally honest.
- **Losing touch with friends:**
  - In the final moments, the value of deep lasting connections becomes clearer, and they wish that they had nurtured those relationships more.

- **Not allowing themselves to be happy:**
  - They realise that happiness is a choice and they should have allowed themselves to experience more joy and not got stuck in limiting beliefs and self-judgement
- **Not taking enough risks**
  - Many regret not stepping out of their comfort zones and taking more risks -whether pursuing their dreams, travelling, or doing what gave them joy. They also realise the reasons for this- fear of failure, rejection, judgments held them back.
- **Neglecting health**
  - They realise that everything in this lifetime must happen through the body, hence the body should have been kept healthy physically, psychologically, and spiritually.
- **Spending too little time with the family**
  - People regretted not making enough memories with the family, friends and people who mattered.

The pre-death period is full of mercy and compassion. If the soul acknowledges, shows compassion, gratitude, forgives and asks for forgiveness, mercy is shown, and the entire process becomes smooth.

The soul is said to receive three pivotal opportunities before it departs from the physical body. This reflects mercy and compassion as the higher beings allow the soul to prepare itself to take on its further journey. These chances may come shortly before death or much earlier, in preparation for death.

Each opportunity is carefully given only if there is a higher purpose, often tied to fulfilling an essential unfinished task, such that the soul may find peace in the astral world. Higher beings operate with wisdom, harmony and understanding. They do not use force. Each one is prepared much in advance according to one's evolution.

We die every day and are reborn every day. Many spiritual, religious, and philosophical traditions consider sleep as a preparation for death. According to Hinduism, the daily cycle of sleep and waking is seen as a metaphor of the cycle of birth, death, and rebirth.

Sleep is a daily cycle of temporary death, withdrawal of consciousness from the external world and the physical body. The consciousness gets transferred to another realm called the astral world or the dream state. A whole lot of activity happens here. This is the state between lifetimes, learning the lessons of the previous lifetime, healing the emotions and thoughts, and preparing for the next lifetime.

According to neuroscience, sleep is the time for the brain to process, heal, and sift memories. The sleep state is divided into many stages. Initially, the activities of the day are processed, and important information is stored according to the associations and conditioning. In the second stage, the healing and renewal process is carried out. In the last stage, the unwanted emotions, fears, and phobias are worked out, and the soul is fed with inspiration. Sleep is an immensely important state where the higher consciousness feeds the soul with new ideas, seed thoughts, new pathways and the breaking down of the knowledge absorbed.

Waking each morning symbolises rebirth; each day is a new day, with renewed body and intentions. It is upon us to make sure that each day is not like the previous day, it is different, new, and there is an incremental positive change in our thoughts, behaviour, and habits. We do not repeat the same mistakes or be in the same vicious cycle. Each day is an opportunity to better ourselves, do incrementally better than yesterday. That is rebirth. Otherwise, we are dying each day without even physically dying. Repeating the same activities and negative emotions of auto mode is akin to death, yet we fear death. If we are not changing, then we are already dead. Dead wood.

The cycle of yugas (Epochs of time according to Hindu Philosophy) represents the rhythm of creation, preservation, and destruction. This is the metaphor for the trinity in many cultures- Brahma, Vishnu and Shiva, or Isis, Horus and Osiris, or God the Father, the Holy Spirit and the Son. There is a similar rhythm in the sleep-wake cycle- As above, so below. Every night is an opportunity to learn, reflect and delete old patterns of limitations. Every morning is a gift of renewal, liberation, and growth.

The spiritual awakening is the rebirth or the 'Waking up" from the sleep of ignorance about one's true consciousness.

The rhythm of life is represented in another way in nature- through seasons. It is a reminder that nothing can be permanent; there has to be death of the old, for the new to take place, if not, we are already dead. In autumn (Fall), leaves change colour, dry up, fall, and decompose. Winter follows, representing dormancy – a time to rest, hibernate, reflect, accumulate resources, time for preparation, a pause, much like sleep. Waking up to spring, nature is reborn, life returns with blooming possibilities. Again, no rose is the same as the last one, no leaf has the same print as the earlier one; there is growth.

Three Questions, Before You Forgive

Forgiveness without truth and honesty is nothing but an empty word. How do we tap into our inner truth while commencing the process of forgiving? It may not be a piece of cake, but these three questions may serve as perfect toolkits to unpack your actual emotions before deciding to go on that journey of forgiveness:

How am I truly feeling inside?

It is normal for us to generally think we are just "angry" or "irritated", forgiveness requires absolute honesty. Dig deeper, delve further into it. Are you feeling betrayed? Do you fear rejection? Are you ashamed? Pinpointing the exact emotion you are experiencing will enable you to see things rationally, rather than spiralling into a vague loop of regret and resentment.

To make this practice simpler, just take a pen and paper to write down the top 3 deep emotions you are feeling. Emotions that are wider than just 'angry'. At any point in time, if you feel you are not able to express your exact feeling, feel free to look up a "wheel of emotions" chart to get a better conclusion. Forgiveness starts with being honest about the wound!

What's the real story?

Every event, every emotion and every feeling has a self-made story behind it. Once you have zeroed in on how you truly feel inside, it's time to hark back to that story you have woven in your mind about the pain. Thoughts like, "My friends disrespected me, they probably don't like me", or "I didn't crack the job interview, I'll not crack any other interview", these are the stories people tend to concoct after trauma.

One must break this chain of creating needless tales in the head. Often, our stories are more toxic than the actual event itself. They kick-start a self-destructive cycle of blame and shame. The easiest way to break the shackles is to write down these toxic stories running in your mind. Read them, and ask yourself: "Is this really the truth, the only possible truth?". Forgiveness empowers us to question the story.

What would I do differently?

This is the ultimate shift. Imagine your life without carrying the burden of that story. Think hard...would it make you feel lighter? Would it help improve your equations with others?

By now, it must have become clear to us that forgiveness doesn't exist with denial. When we reframe the story to a more positive approach, we are reclaiming the energy we wasted on obsessing over things that didn't matter. Forgiveness enables us to release pain and retain freedom!

All It Takes…is 15 Minutes!

A pre-sleep ritual is powerful for setting up for a restful sleep and a fresh beginning to the next day. Building this habit is an investment in a healthy body, cellular repair, clearing the thoughts cache, and a restored, clear mind.

Here is a pre-sleep routine suggestion:

1. Switch off social media, TV or any other kind of screen time which can interfere with your brain waves, eyes and thoughts. What you consume socially also sits in your aura and does not get digested by the mind. The stimulation of distractions can make it harder for the body and mind to wind down.
2. What you consume before sleep is food for the brain in the resting period, hence read uplifting, spiritual, inspiring, self-growth books before you plan to wind down. If you don't like to read, try a few paragraphs; the exercise will help the brain to slow down. Reading will help navigate the thoughts towards positivity and growth.
3. Reflect on the day, notice lessons learnt, small joys, and any areas of growth. Mentally erase the areas which look negative.
4. Create a holographic movie in the mind where you, as an observer, are looking at yourself enacting the day. Guide yourself to erase the part where you think you have gone wrong, and then recreate the same part, doing the right thing. Feel the positive emotions in your body when you do the right thing.
5. Follow this with acknowledging three positive things about yourself. Write this in a diary and collate different aspects each day.

6. Practice forgiveness by gently forgiving yourself for any mistakes. Then, forgive and release tensions, grudges, and anger from the past. This step is crucial to empty the trash bin of emotions, such that every day is lighter, new and fresh.
   - "I forgive myself for any intentional or unintentional judgement, criticism or hurt towards self or others. I forgive everyone (or a specific name) for any hurt, grudge, resentment, judgement or any negative towards me".
   - "I release all the negative thoughts. I bless others with love, peace, growth, success, and good health. I allow positivity to flow into me and from me. With gratitude and compassion."
7. Express gratitude towards everything you have been given, and you want to manifest, as if it's already been provided.
   "Every cell in my body is filled with peace, compassion towards myself, everyone and everything, gratitude towards what has been given with grace. I am the creator of happiness, peace and abundance"
8. Affirm positive suggestions to your brain before sleeping to shift the energy towards creating new possibilities.
   - "I am in the right place, with infinite resources, at the right time, manifesting my highest potential with grace"
   - "I am guided by my highest purpose, perfectly aligned and positioned with my life's path, manifesting my best potential smoothly"
   - "I am gliding through life with confidence, knowing the universe is aligning the right opportunities, people and timing to fulfil my highest purpose"

- "I receive my gifts and fully align with my higher purpose with joy"
- "I receive my superpowers with grace"

The sleep routine may seem detailed and long; however, with practice, it becomes easy and takes fifteen minutes. Think of it as an intention where each night you are setting the stage for your rebirth. Embrace this time as a gift you give yourself as you prepare your body and mind to work with superpowers.

Every stage of your life will call out a small version of you, which is new, different, and more powerful than the earlier one. Nature, through life, crafts the conditions for your growth. You need to walk the path to bring out the new version of you.

Another way to consciously slip into the state of awakened sleep is through meditation. With the right technique, continuous practice and building a habit, practitioners can feel the consciousness expanding beyond the limitations of the physical body, into the realms where even sleep and death cannot go. The practice involves training the body to be calm, withdrawal of the awareness from the senses to the breath and then to a singular point, stillness of the mind.

Every practice of meditation offers a different experience; there are good days and excellent days. You can see light, then a dark tunnel, then the expansion of light. Expansion of consciousness can take you to different realms where intuition can be heightened. When I began my journey, I used to get premonitions of people I would meet, to such a degree that the colour and pattern of their clothes would be exactly what I would see much earlier.

Over a period of practice, I did not see anything real; I thought the magic was lost. It was just a promotion to magical lights and different dimensions of awareness. Accessing intuition, guidance, and support for the direction in life becomes easier. However, to enhance the power of intuition, emotional purification is a prerequisite and forgiveness is one of the vital secrets.

It may not sound easy, as this superpower truly renews you. Forgiveness frees us to move forward with clarity, reclaiming the energy which must have been tied up in grudges, resentment or hurt. It gives the control back to you to focus on what truly matters. Neuroscience shows that forgiveness reshapes the brain's wiring. This is not about ignoring the past; it's about breaking the vicious, redundant cycle. It is the ultimate inner strength.

Once we realise why we forgive and understand how we forgive, we are equipped with a superpower like no other, one that can lift a mountainload worth of weight off our shoulders. Once we imbibe and master the art of forgiveness, the fourth and final superpower becomes the frontier we must chase next.

The Fourth Super Power

SERVICE

Living On Purpose

"The human being has a unique place among God's creation. "I breathed into him my Spirit," God says. Each one of us, without exception, is designed to be God's delegate on earth. Ask yourself, just how often do you behave like a delegate, if you ever do so? Remember, it falls upon each of us to discover the divine spirit inside and live by it."

– ***Shams-E-Tabrizi***

Humans are distinguished from other species by their ability to connect, and with the divine. We are not merely physical beings; we create thoughts, connect through emotions and are fitted with programs of higher purpose. Humans have a unique position in creation; we have a responsibility to represent the divine in the physical form through intentions, spoken words, and habits. This responsibility is a call, a call to discover the superpower which awakens the divine within us. That super power is -Service.

Service is a foundational value, telling us to always work with awareness. It is the intention to do the greater good in every act. It is to set an objective in the mind, that whatever is done by humans must be for the good of self and others. It is to avoid doing things just for ourselves, which may or may not be good for others. It is to refrain from doing things just for others, which may or may not be good for ourselves.

Service is not just a feeling or an emotion; it is where the action lies. While feelings of gratitude, compassion and forgiveness inspire us, these must go further to transform into tangible action. Service bridges the gap between feeling and doing, embodying the principle of 'walking the talk.' It defines who just talks, and who steps out of the zone, takes a step, and aligns the thought with action to live authentically.

People who think, say and act differently are fighting within. They are not grounded or aligned with their core. When there is war going on inside, one is consumed with lower emotions such as anxiety, need to control, stress, ego, stubbornness, unawareness, emotional blocks, etc. This results in a different outcome from what one set as a goal. It starts a vicious cycle of blaming the circumstances.

We are flooded with knowledge; however, how many of us end up acting on it? Knowing something and not acting on it is the perfect cage you can set for yourself. Making effort and acting in alignment with the highest intention sets you free. It is liberating when you don't have to pretend to know everything, yet you take baby steps towards the values.

The focus should not be on the outcome, but rather the process! This transcends the ego and its desires. "What's in it for me?" or "Why should I do this?" is the dilemma of humanity, and it must be put to rest. What you get out of doing the right thing is intangible. It cannot be put into any value or a reward. The difference between people who talk and those who do not talk is the intention of service. Authenticity is a value that can be measured by actions.

Service is not just a higher ground moral choice; it is a tangible and forceful tool for evolution, a breakthrough edge for growth. There is a preset formula for 'Success' laid down since the time of Darwin: Survival of the fittest. Since then, humanity has been in a perpetual competitive survival mode. In reality, the switch from survive to thrive is through a pure altruistic way.

Science suggests that doing things which help us and others, without any ulterior motive, assists the process of evolution. Nature is not a blanket standard; it is diverse, and each organism is different. Each species has a different ecosystem, challenges and weaknesses. Evolution can only happen if we collectively support each other. Service is an opportunity, an invitation to participate in the collaborative effort of growth. It is a choice to cooperate in collective happiness, rather than choosing competition as a road to success. In the end, we must think about who exactly does individual success serve?

When we give, protect and nurture ourselves and others, the latent power of interconnectedness gets activated. Why would organisms "choose" to help others at their own expense? By sharing resources, protecting the vulnerable, and fostering the young, we are improving our own prospects as a species.

Trees, for example, through an intricate network of underground fungi share nutrients, directing resources toward weakened or young trees who might otherwise struggle to survive.

Cats, wolves, elephants, and so on, also nurture the young ones of other mothers when they are absent or unable to take care, ensuring that the next generation has a fighting chance.

Helping someone, not out of pity, but rather out of genuine cooperation, is an instinct. Notice that children are quick to help when someone is struggling with a task or emotions. Their approach is spontaneous, joyful, and free from any expectations. They don't consider including others, sharing things or showing love as an obligation or duty. It is pure joy.

As we grow older, that simple instinct to just be of help gets buried beneath layers of expectations, disappointment, and doubt. The childlike spirit of genuineness is worn down by the people around us telling us not to be a nice person. There are times we helped and received nothing in return, we felt taken advantage of or faced constant questioning from people around. "What are you getting out of this?" or "You are wasting your time helping others." These voices chip away at the honest drive, and gradually the heart begins to harden, looking out for one's needs because the mind is convinced that it is foolish to help others.

The open-hearted generosity, free-flowing spirit, and purity of intention turn into guarded scepticism, conditioned by the world that equates giving and getting in return.

Hearts are further hardened, shut down by technology, which is making humanity detached. The illusion of connecting people is isolating. Convenience and minimal effort are fading the human touch, genuine conversations, and empathy. Technology and innovations are supposed to free us from mundane tasks so that we can focus on what really matters, for example, building communities towards development, finding sustainable solutions to problems, and utilising time to connect with people. Instead, we are cut off and isolated.

For example, dating was once filled with anticipation and the thrill of real encounters, but adventure has become an endless cycle of swipes and ghosting. People are more disposable than gadgets. Technology is seducing us, screen time is the new drug, speed is the new currency, and instant gratification is the new value.

There is overwhelming evidence that links excessive smartphone and social media usage to interpersonal costs. Frontier, one of Switzerland's leading research publishers, in an article discussing "addictive disorders", states that phone usage during social interactions ("phubbing") is said to harm relationship quality and well-being, while problematic smartphone usage patterns also relate to aggression dynamics.

In an ideal world, when technology finds solutions, it should create more time for humans to bring out the superpower- the power of showing up for one another, the ability to connect deeply and meaningfully, creating an environment where others feel safe, seen and valued. The invitation of service is to offer our presence in any given moment without past baggage, future worries or any judgment. It's about creating a space that smells of authenticity and openness. A place where there are no defences, personal walls, or guards. What makes humans unique is the ability to communicate and understand through emotions.

Why is humanity all of a sudden more lonely, anxious, depressed, angry or at war? The BMJ medical journal's systematic review covering 113 countries opined that "problematic levels of loneliness are experienced by a substantial proportion of the population".

Clearly, this is a direct result of the disconnection with the self. Because we are run by algorithms, automation, and digital solutions. We are keeping up with the fake rush, optimising every experience. While productivity may be improving, the concepts of empathy and warmth need to be reintroduced in our lifestyles.

Artificial intelligence is capable of diagnosing diseases, predicting behaviour, creating music, and manufacturing art. It is expertly predicting human likes and dislikes; however, it cannot replicate the deep compassionate essence of eye contact, physical hugs, and a reassuring touch on the shoulders. Things that state-someone has your back!

As we rush into becoming a hyper-individualised society, "success" is increasingly defined as personal gain. Soon, we will be pushed to a corner where the value of the experiences that make us human will be more recognised and appreciated.

The preference towards non-curated and non-AI experiences is coming sooner than we know! A 2025 Ernst & Young report indicates there is "growing user fatigue with the current generation of AI," noting that AI-generated content "feels sterile and disconnected from real human experience".

At present, though, as AI threatens to overtake humans in many careers, service is the answer to growing insecurity from technology advancement encroaching on job security. As routine tasks and micromanagement are taken over by technology, the role of service becomes more crucial. Leadership today is not just strategy, metrics or output; it is about supporting, guiding, and inspiring employees. The focus shifts to creating a workplace where individuals feel connected, heard, appreciated, and motivated to come to the space and not work from home.

Beyond the transactional exchange of giving, there is also mentoring as a service. It's about selfless commitment to someone else's growth and potential. It's not just about transferring skills or expertise, which even tech can do! When we shift the focus to service as an intention, it brings in trust, encouragement, and a vision. A mentor has to be a guide who genuinely invests in another's journey. It is a cycle of support and growth. When a company is built on advanced tech, yet rooted in serving the customer as well as employees, it gains a unique strength.

Service doesn't just help us on an emotional level; it also uplifts our mental health. Always ask yourself, what are you feeding your nervous system? One of the best wholesome ways to keep the nervous system happy is 'helping others'.

Research says there is something called 'Helper's high'- a natural, brain and body boosting high post any genuine act of service. This is more potent than a "runner's high", because the "Helper's High" releases a powerful concoction of chemicals or hormones like:

- **Dopamine**: Every time you lend a helping hand, make a positive impact, dopamine kicks in to reward you- "That felt good, let's do it again"- it's a cycle of brain-do-positive-get rewarded-do it again.
- **Oxytocin**: When you help someone, the connection you feel is because of the 'Love Hormone'- Oxytocin. It relaxes the

nervous system and makes you feel safe and secure. The social bond is strengthened.

- **Serotonin**: It is your inbuilt sunshine, 'The mood regulator'. This hormone reduces stress, anxiety, and depression. Makes you feel mentally tough.
- **Endorphins**: The default, natural painkillers are released when we help others, building an emotional armour for us such that we don't feel isolated or lonely.

"For it is in giving that we receive"

– St Francis of Asisi

There is a seed of reciprocity in service! We are given a lot because we need to share, and on the other hand, what we need, we must share, even if it's a small amount. Hermetic philosophy talks about the core principles on which nature is based. According to it, the principle of cause-and-effect states that nothing happens by chance; every action we take sets a cause in motion, which brings about the effect. When we understand that every action has an effect, we understand that giving is not really about helping someone else. It is about sowing seeds which will, whether we want or not, bear the same fruits of generosity, which we must receive.

"The Principle of Rhythm" explains the natural law of the cyclical flow of giving and receiving. Everything moves in cycles-day turns into night, winter turns into spring, ocean returns to the shore, every breath flows in and out, there is a sleep and wake cycle, circadian rhythm, and menstrual cycle. Giving and receiving are part of the same cycle; it is natural, and one cannot exist without the other. Both create harmony. If we try to take without giving, or only give without allowing ourselves to receive, the natural flow is disrupted. We need to identify if we are giving enough and allowing ourselves to receive the infinite abundance of everything available to us.

The Hermetic principle of Gender is a concept that says everything contains both "Masculine" and "Feminine" aspects. Giving is associated with the active, outward flow of energy, which is masculine. Receiving, in contrast, is passive, open, surrender, allowing things to come to us, very feminine energy.

This is a concept which is present in many cultures and known by different names. For example, the concept of Yin and Yang in China, or Purush and Prakriti in Hinduism. The masculine and feminine are not separate, rather interconnected and interdependent. The yin-yang symbol shows each as a half circle, with a dot of the opposite within it, symbolising that each contains the seed of the other. These energies must be in harmony to create balance with nature and our bodies. Too much passive, i.e. receiving without giving, will create stagnation, and too much giving activity and dynamism will lead to burnout. Masculine is action and support, feminine is accepting help, kindness, and abundance.

In society today, there is an imbalance of yin and yang energies. Women are over extending their yang powers by giving, and men are not recognising their yin, which is nurturing and receptive. This has happened over generations, with women displaying self-sacrifice and men being emotionally arid. A systematic review and meta-analysis by ScienceDirect concluded that female caregivers, compared to male caregivers, report higher burden, lower well-being, and greater physical health impacts, reflecting generations of women's overextension. Whereas, a cross-sectional study of Indian men (aged 19 to 65) found high rates of emotional suppression tied to traditional masculine norms.

Nature has its own remarkable way of balancing through extreme or challenging situations, which put humans in a situation where they are pushed towards learning, growth and change. For example, economic instability, pandemic, emotional or mental health crisis, etc have forced humanity to look at the stereotypical traditional roles, reevaluate and reawaken them.

When Life is Shared

Meera often felt invisible. She worked tirelessly — kids' homework, groceries, meals, laundry — while her husband, Raj, came home late, expecting dinner and a quiet atmosphere. The weight of unspoken expectations left her feeling less and unappreciated.

One Sunday, Raj was about to park himself on a sofa when he noticed her sitting silently, staring at the wall, while the milk on the burner was about to spill. While switching off the burner, he said, "Let me handle the dinner tonight." The kids looked up in surprise.

This small act broke a long pattern. The following week, Raj began picking up groceries on his way home and occasionally cooking a meal. Meera felt lighter; kindness was no longer one-sided, it became love in action. She felt valued and supported.

Balance Before Burnout

"An empty lantern provides no light. Self-care is the fuel that allows your light to shine brightly."

– Anonymous

"How can I be of help to others?" is the first question that comes up when we think of service. As a society, we have romanticised ideas of pushing through and playing martyrs while glorifying self-denial and sacrifice. Self-care is scoffed at as a selfish luxury.

There will always be a fall guy (or girl)- the one who will give and give endlessly, because they have been conditioned never to take, always be the bigger person. The unspoken rule, or the underlying message, is that other people's needs are bigger and more important. It becomes a loop; the more they give, the more responsibilities they get, and they wear it as a badge of honor garbed in virtue. Such people endure quietly, just doing what is expected.

There are consequences of giving more than receiving. The cup, once full, slowly becomes empty. They don't realise this, and they don't even stop to check, because there is an underlying rule that pausing for self-care is selfish- almost an act of weakness or irresponsibility. Thus, eventually, their reserves empty out.

Then, one fine day, when the reserves have vanished, they realise something is wrong. Their energy is low, they have no motivation, and are constantly irritable. Even then, they end up feeling guilty for feeling empty! Unfortunately, they believe that this is the time to push harder and endure longer. They feel that pushing harder will help them seem like people who are strong under pressure. That is how the invisible resentment, frustration and depression start to build inside!

It won't appear as loud anger, but rather a slow burn in the body, with signs such as pain, exhaustion, emotional breakdown, brain fog, and a sense of being overwhelmed even by small things. This internal chaos is often unseen and overlooked till it comes out as a massive disease.

USA's PubMed Central houses an article that talks about the "caregiver burden." The article analyses that caregivers who devote extensive time and energy to the service of others, while seldom caring about themselves, become prime candidates for decreased quality of life and experiencing deterioration in physical and psychological health, with common reports of depression, anger, anxiety, and guilt. Over 50% of family carers report chronic health issues (e.g., hypertension, heart problems) and, sadly, often delay or avoid seeking care for themselves.

Service does emanate from sacrifice as a virtue; however, sacrifice per se has been misrepresented, misappropriated, and misused by many cultures. Throughout history, it has been presented as giving up personal needs, desires, and even one's identity, to make others happy or to please the authority. This kind of sacrifice promotes suppression, disempowerment, even abuse of power and makes belief authority.

Sacrifice is a virtue which emerges from the higher self for spiritual and personal growth. It is not about giving up your authentic self; it is about sacrificing the lower unproductive parts of ourselves, it's about sacrificing resistance to change, it is about surrendering the fear, worry, need to control and guilt.

A highly secret concept called 'The Causal body' is taught in higher levels of evolution in many traditions. It is the home to the various bodies- the higher self, mental, astral, etheric and the physical body. Renowned author Arthur E. Powell's comprehensive works describe "The Causal Body" as "the vehicle of the Human Soul" that exists at a higher vibrational level than physical, etheric, astral, and mental bodies. The Welsh Theosophist states that the "development of the Mental, Astral and Physical Bodies depends upon the building of the Causal Body. There is, in fact, no complete Human being until this body is complete."

In simple words, the Causal body is the container in which the body resides. It holds 'The cause' or the blueprint of the reason why we are here in this incarnation on earth. It has the 'Akashic Records', hence also the 'Karma' of all the past lives. It is a spiritual repository sending us the strengths built up through lifetimes and guiding us through the virtues we need to master in this lifetime. The Causal Body sends information about lessons to be learned, wisdom we have gathered and karma to be worked out through experiences, people, situations, personality gifts and constant reminders to the path of higher purpose. It holds the purpose of the soul in various lifetimes, much like a mentor who can see a rookie's future. It is said that, in order to develop a clear link to the intuition provided by the causal body, one must develop three key qualities: Knowledge, Sacrifice and Love. Let's explore these three aspects a bit further:

Let go!

In the truest sense, **"Sacrifice"** is about giving up the lower nature that clouds our thinking with negative habits, behaviour, and thoughts. Most cultures promote sacrifice at a physical level by fasting or by offerings to the fire. However, emotional, mental and spiritual sacrifice is to consciously choose the higher emotion, thought and desire. It means we must let go of attachments which are temporary. To not let our worth be tied to things which reflect success and have power over us.

Desires, in themselves, are powerful emotions which motivate humans to grow. However, desires of wanting more, when rooted in a sense of competition, or a feeling of lack, pride, or the need for external validation, will lead to emptiness and a constant state of hustle. It is not about giving up desires; it is about sacrificing a lower desire for a higher purpose of service. Sacrifice is not about losing one's identity or denying one's needs. It is choosing what truly serves at a higher level in the long term. That vision and clarity are developed with knowledge and awareness.

Alice Ann Bailey, and one of the most influential figures in 20th-century New Age spirituality, emphasises that true sacrifice is selfless service, done not out of obligation or fear, but out of a deep sense of unity with all life. By practising this type of sacrifice, a person purifies the lower aspects of themselves and begins to align more with the divine purpose.

Sacrifice the comfort which keeps you in a loop and does not allow change or growth. Sacrifice what you already know to make space for a bigger and more powerful truth. Sacrifice laziness in the body, emotions, and thoughts. Sacrifice lower, smaller, short-term pleasures for bigger dreams which have a long-term impact.

Sacrifice, judging the situation, person and yourself based on your understanding of the truth. Replace it with understanding that life is dynamic and your perspective is not the only way to look at the world. Sacrifice small-mindedness and bring in the belief that you are worthy of more, should you choose to claim it with faith. Sacrifice cruelty, pride, hatred, dislikes, comparison, harmfulness, maliciousness, and more such thoughts and actions.

Sacrifice your resistance to change. Sacrifice the need to be like others, to fit in, to blend and do what is always done. Sacrifice the status quo! Sacrifice the need to hustle to succeed. Sacrifice distractions coming in the way of your purpose. Sacrifice the need to know more and act less. Sacrifice the mindset that you know it all. Sacrifice all that is lying around in the body and mind, making you stale and self-destructive.

Glance within

Knowledge is the second key aspect to be developed. It is of various kinds. Intellectual knowledge is good; however, there is so much information around that it has polarised the minds.

Opinions have divided people, and as they continue to hold on to their beliefs, they are isolating themselves.

Technology is supposed to usher in knowledge and build communities; however, there is more loneliness and wars in this tech-enabled world. This is because we are living in echo chambers, where our own thoughts are reflected by algorithms.

Alice Bailey, in the 1800's, pre-empted this and talked about the need for discernment- the ability to discern truth from illusion through mental clarity and awareness. This higher knowledge is gained through understanding the true self, the nature of the soul, laws of the universe.

Discernment was first proposed by Budha which is critical thinking. Master Choa, founder of Modern Pranic Healing and Arhatic Yoga, emphasised discernment as a key virtue to develop a sharp mind. When they say knowledge is power, in today's times, discernment is power.

Knowledge is static, amassing information which may not be of any use, discernment is dynamic: questioning the assumptions, building self-trust, removing superstition or blind faith, reducing dependence on an external locus of control. Discernment is an active wheel of knowledge, constantly evolving, filtering, and analysing to provide clarity and quick self-empowered decisions.

In today's times, the only way to gain power, sell a concept or a product, and control society's mind to behave in a certain way, is by bombarding information which will control the process of thinking and behaviour. Humans are too lazy to think for themselves; they would rather choose a basic number of likes, subscriptions, followers, reviews, or anything that is validated by external factors.

The highest form of knowledge is the awareness of our true self, peeling the essence of who we are, including physical attributes, emotional aspects and intellect. Self-awareness is the power that will filter the important from the useless, propelling you to enable subtle transformation. One must use self-awareness to go within and gain knowledge about strengths, motivations and joys. Be aware of the triggers, fears, guilts, and judgments. Seek more information on how to overcome these. Identify patterns that hold you back from living your authentic self with ease.

When you know your true self, you will go beyond your ego, labels or identity which others want to see. You will be liberated from unwarranted expectations and the external loop of pressure. This will reflect in relationships, which most of the time are projections of one's own expectations. The knowledge that every human is unique, we are interconnected and what you do to others reflects how you see yourself, will have a transformational effect on your relations with people.

All heart

The third quality to connect with the causal body is **love**. Do not mistake this for the hackneyed romance or lust wrapped in a word called love. Real love is the most powerful force that binds us to the higher purpose, our inner self with the outside world. It is the connecting force between people; it is by far the highest of all emotions! It thus includes gratitude, compassion, forgiveness, and service. It is that force which has the ability to transmute the lower self into a very successful higher version of self.

Love is the bridge between the physical world and the higher consciousness, because it has the magic to dissolve the ego. When you care about something or someone, you break all barriers to achieve it. Love can collapse past, present and future and takes one beyond the physical boundaries. Love is the fuel that has the force to propel dreams into reality. Those who manifest faster are full of love for self and others. It is the secret ingredient to clarity of mind, intuition, foresight, and success.

Love, in its various avatars, is magic, it is just a concept, an idea, a theoretical answer until you do something with it. It doesn't become real until something is done; it needs to be put into action. Master Choa describes service as love in motion.

We have two parts to us- the lower self and the higher self. The lower self belongs to the ego- tied down by ego, fears, insecurities, and the need to fiercely protect the bubble of comfort. The higher self, on the other hand, is about purpose, growth, innovation, ideas, connection, and vision. It is the part of self that sees the bigger picture, long-term impact.

Knowledge helps us discern what is feeding the ego and what is the larger viewpoint. This knowledge becomes real as love steps in; it is the bridge between the lower and the higher self. Love operates from the higher self and defines the purpose, your divine nature and essence. It creates the drive to work towards the purpose relentlessly, makes work sound like play, and creates the motivation to let go of small stuff and serve something greater.

Without love, work seems like a chore; with love, every action is service towards oneself.

When you are truly coming from love, you disappear, and the service makes fear, insecurity, doubt, fade away- what is left is pure joy of the flow. The action of service is proof that love exists. Wisdom can only be achieved through love. Love cannot be perfected in the mind. It must be actioned through service. Hence, service is the highway to wisdom.

Once these three keys have been unlocked, your understanding of service and the way you apply it in the real world will radically change for the better.

"Prayer in action is love, love in action is service"

– Mother Teresa

Service begins with self, when your cup overflows and you can fill others with love, compassion and as an intention to pass on the blessings. At a concrete stage, self service begins with fulfilling the needs of the body, it is your vehicle in this life and shows up every day. To serve this incredible, irreplaceable machine, one must:

- Give it rest, much like recharging the batteries of a phone. Every day over a million cells die in the human body, and equal numbers are produced. To achieve this remarkable feat, resting the body physically, emotionally and mentally is a must.

- Nutrition is nourishment for the body. What you put in is what you get. If you sow a papaya seed, you will not get mangoes. Hence, be careful of how you are nourishing your body.
- Movement in any form is fuel for the body.
- Breathwork is the secret to an energised body. Slow, rhythmic breathing from the belly is the key; it fills the entire body with energy.

It's not just our physical body! The Emotional body is also a new reality. Serving the physical body and ignoring the emotional body is hara-kiri. To serve our emotional body, we must:

- Identify the patterns of emotions, feelings and triggers behind negative emotions.
- Understand that every negative feeling has an origin in some inability.
- Observe the patterns and situations without being biased. Acknowledge your emotions before reacting. Go deeper and ask yourself why you are reacting. This will show the underlying cause of the inability to respond and the urgent need to react.
- Find the unmet need, void or what you expect out of yourself in the moment,
- Fill the void with the right expression, habit, thoughts, or change in behaviour.

You think about sixty thousand thoughts a day, and most of them are not doing any favour. Negative thoughts are tiny droplets, eroding your confidence, self-esteem and courage. Self service is to:

- Create a positive personality and a vision in the head which is a blueprint for reality
- Challenge the negative self-talk and replace it with self-compassion, appreciation, and respect.
- Replace criticism, judgment, and guilt with gratitude to rewire the brain.

You are not just the body; you are being spiritually fed by the nutrition of ideas and purpose. Investing in self- growth and development is a big service to oneself because that is the key to keeping us connected to the authentic self. Always remember to:

- Keep yourself abreast with new concepts, ideas, scientific data about nutrition, mobility, psychology, and ways to minimise stress
- Take time off in solitude to connect with your deepest self. Ask yourself challenging questions. You need not find the answers.
- Do things that give you deep joy, fulfilment and nourish your soul, and not short-term pleasures which you may regret soon.
- Pursue the quest of purpose and the intention behind everything. Remember the service to self is to fulfil the desires through the highest intentions and not die with guilt, remorse or lack.
- Get out of your comfort zone to make connections with the higher self through stillness, meditation, breathwork, and so on. Make time to understand things beyond your sphere, such as energy, aura, manifestation, etc.

Everyone has been given unique gifts. These have no meaning in isolation. Those gifts must be shared to complement each other. A fruit vendor cannot do the work of a dentist, and vice versa. A world filled only with fruit vendors or dentists would be unsustainable. The reason behind our gifts is to fulfil individual purpose, and to connect and contribute to society. Service is an opportunity to bring the gifts together and contribute as a community. It is the superpower that can connect people and collectively uplift humanity.

More Than Mere Duty

"Recognise the Lord in all, and you will serve all."

– Guru Nanak

Great leaders, thinkers, saints, and messiahs spread the message of oneness and embodied it by serving others. A rookie joining a big company starts with the basic tasks and must prove himself to move ahead. As he accomplishes the given tasks, he is given more. They don't begin as leaders, rather through hard work, dedication and learning they become leaders, inspiring others. Saints and spiritual teachers were no different.

Jesus Christ, Sai Baba, Sri Yukteshwargiri, Lahiri Mahasaya, Guru Nanak, and many others like them had one thing in common. Their miracles were not about showing power- they were motivational presentations to instil faith in something greater, beyond the physical world, a divine force that holds everything together. Through their acts of service, they gave a glimpse of purpose to everyone. The purpose is to take responsibility for your life and serve the larger society with love.

Jesus performed many healing miracles and even resurrected. Sai Baba of Shirdi cured people of leprosy by just giving them his shawl. Shri Guru Nanak Devji is known for miraculous interventions such as purifying poisoned food, calming a storm, and saving people from harm. Mother Teresa felt deeply committed to serve those no one else would. Sri Yukteshwar Giri, one of the teachers of Shri Paramhamsa Yogananda, miraculously cured his disciples. Shri Yogananda admitted that Sri Yukteswar told him, "Medicines have limitations; the creative life-force has none," after which Yogananda's chronic dyspepsia vanished.

All these figures didn't wake up one day and think "Let's care for the world." They had awakened to the truth that the only purpose is to connect and contribute. They are a continuous living reminder that service is the highest quality.

Leaders are the modern-day saints; they prioritise serving others and thereby empowering individuals, and assimilating them into a community of unique individuals working together for a common goal, fostering collaboration and enabling collective needs. This brings us to the idea of leaders functioning as mediums to serve, or, in basic terms, the idea of 'Servant as Leader'.

The concept of 'Servant as Leader' was first conceptualised by Robert K Greenleaf in 1970, defining his leadership approach as serving first, sharing power, fostering growth and community building. Traditional leadership focused on authority, power, or hierarchy, service leadership stems from the purpose of collaboration and empathy, but Greenleaf's vision centred on the idea that great leaders are great servants first.

Service leadership is critical today because of the rapidly changing landscape of the workforce. There is more self-awareness in the workplace, as well as the need to be recognised in team members. Today, in any organisation, authenticity is the default currency, and inclusivity is not an effort- it's a pre-requisite. Finally, purpose-driven action is the default setting. Millennials and Gen Z prioritise purpose- they want to work for organisations and leaders who care.

Offices cannot be aloof from challenges that the world is facing, e.g. climate change, mental health, or women's empowerment. On these lines, service leadership focuses on listening, empowering, and taking collective action. Ultimately, organisations are fertile lands to check social inequalities, and hence, creating a sustainable environment and promoting equal voice is not just ethical, but rather smart business.

We can exemplify this further by exploring a story.

Arjun was a difficult client, always nitpicking, sending late-night emails, and criticising the vendor team no matter how much they delivered. The vendors dreaded his calls.

One morning, rushing across the street to grab a coffee before his meeting, Arjun almost stepped into traffic when a motorbike came speeding toward him. A hand pulled him back just in time. Startled, he turned- it was Rohit, the very vendor he had been berating for weeks. That afternoon, instead of firing off another set of harsh words,

Arjun said, "I realise I've been tough. I truly appreciate your effort. Let's work as partners"

An undeniable fact is that everyone is serving someone! Employees serve employers or their organisation by contributing skills and time. Employers serve employees by providing opportunities, resources, and support. Employees also serve clients or brands by offering products and services. Brands serve consumers by meeting their needs. Consumers serve brands by enabling growth and loyalty.

Parents serve children by nurturing and guiding them. Children serve parents by bringing joy and fulfilment. Governments serve people by ensuring safety, justice, infrastructure, and opportunities. People serve the government by paying taxes, abiding by the law, and participating in democracy. People serve the nation by contributing to economic and cultural growth. A nation serves people by providing identity, belonging, land and a shared purpose.

Service is the invisible thread that binds us. This cycle of service is the fabric of cultures, nations, and civilisations. The moment this stops, there are wars, coups, unrest, and the disintegration of values. Relationships are essentially about service- not in a servile sense, rather an act of showing up with our best selves to honour the connection we share with the other person. At their core, relationships are all about nurturing the foundational values of trust, respect, love and mutual growth.

Service can be broadly understood by taking a look at Indian spirituality and history, too. Hanuman, one of the Hindu Gods, is often depicted with the picture of Lord Rama and Sita in his heart, depicting unwavering devotion and faith, which is a higher form of love. According to Hindu scriptures, when Lord Rama asked Hanuman how he perceived him, Hanuman replied, "When I think I am the body, I am your servant, when I identify with my soul, I am part of you, and when I realise my true self, we are one."

Hanuman represents the physical existence of humans with the body, emotions and mind, whose sole purpose is to be a faithful servant of the higher self or the higher potential- represented by Lord Rama. The body, emotions and mind are instruments of action. The journey of every individual is reflected by Hanuman's unwavering devotion and faith in the dharma- right job to be done in the moment by removing inner obstacles.

Just like an average human being, Hanuman did not know his potential until he put his faith and acted upon things, e.g. lifting the mountain, crossing the ocean, burning the palace, etc. His intention, devotion and faith unfolded his power.

When Life is Shared

"The meeting of two personalities is like the contact of two chemical substances: if there is any reaction, both are transformed."

– Carl Jung

Relationships may start with something external, such as a need for companionship, love, attraction and emotional support, but over time they naturally evolve. If they don't, there is stagnation. Much like chemical compounds, they retain the essence of individuals however, transform into something new when they come together. Just like compounds have a specific characteristic that elements on their own do not possess. At the same time, too much of one element or an unstable combination can lead to a volatile mix.

While it is common for relationships to sometimes fall into an unhealthy dynamic where one person gives too much, thinking serving the other is the only way to continue the harmony, the other takes it in without reciprocation. Burnout, resentment, and disconnection is the result of this dynamic.

Part of the issue lies in the way we have been conditioned to always give and never ask, specifically when trying to fit into certain predefined stereotyped roles and the expectations. While playing the role, one tends to lose one's self-identity and instead match up to expectations. This is good as well as bad, good because one does things beyond one's capacity, bad because it is expected every time, and in the end, overextension of oneself kills authenticity. The 'Provider' and the 'Caretaker' roles are interchangeable, and cannot be played by one person all the time.

Yin and yang is how one can describe this- yin is receptivity, allowance, receiving nurturing and softness, while yang represents giving, action, assertiveness, and strength. The balance between yin and yang cannot be equally split all the time; an understanding of the situation can help. When there is a yin mode, it is all taking- there is a struggle for control or attention. If both are in the giving mode, they might neglect their own needs, leading to resentment, unspoken dissatisfaction or something like that.

One of the main intentions in a relationship is to honour the space, trust and commitment shared between the two partners. It is not about expecting to change the other to make a mirror image of yourself. In a garden, no two roses are the same. The beauty lies in bringing two different beings together in harmony, and not creating uniformity. To serve a partnership, one need not fix it; instead, celebrate the diversity, adding to the richness, creating a safe, nurturing environment.

Service, in a relationship, comes as a commitment to complement the other in more ways than one. It signifies putting in an effort, understanding your partner, and loving them in a way that a union achieves the maximum human potential. A potential which they wouldn't have been able to reach individually.

Meera, a hardworking homemaker, often felt invisible in the very home she made. She worked tirelessly- kids' homework, groceries, meals, laundry- while on the other hand, her husband, Raj, came home late, expecting a freshly cooked dinner and a quiet atmosphere. The weight of unspoken expectations left Meera feeling less and unappreciated.

It all changed one Sunday, when Raj was about to park himself on a sofa. He noticed his wife sitting silently, staring at the wall, while the milk on the burner was about to spill. Switching off the burner, he said, "Let me handle the dinner tonight." The kids looked up in surprise!

This small act broke a long pattern. The following week, Raj began picking up groceries on his way home and occasionally cooking a meal. Meera felt lighter; kindness was no longer one-sided, it became love in action. She felt valued and supported.

Raising, Not Owning

"Your children are not your children. They are the sons & daughters of Life's longing for itself. They come through you, but not from you, though they are with you, they belong not to you."

– Kahlil Gibran

Children are nature's gift to this world- beings of immense potential who have intelligently, strategically chosen to be here in a particular family, to certain parents, in a place and nation where they will be guided, helped, protected, and inspired to achieve their unique purpose.

Raising a child is akin to nurturing a plant- children are like seeds, each carrying a blueprint of an exceptional tree. The environment in which the tree will be nurtured determines the fruit.

As parents, teachers and caregivers, the role is not to control or own the child, or to try to fulfil through them the dreams one could not achieve. The child comes with a default blueprint; the job of the environment is to nurture this embedded purpose, such that it is achieved seamlessly.

The notion of controlling or owning children stems from cultural and personal expectations. Parents may unconsciously project their unfulfilled ambitions onto their children, hoping to find validation, pride, and achievement through their success. Children in many ways are not job lists or projects to be completed with competing fierceness.

Children give birth to wisdom in parents by pushing them to be aware of their latent fears, insecurities, and limitations. Parenting is a humble reminder that actions speak louder than words. Action is the ultimate tool of love, knowledge, sacrifice and trust.

John always believed that "providing for his daughter" meant paying the bills and securing a good future for her. But, during a parent-teacher meeting, he learned that she was being body-shamed by classmates and was struggling silently. That day, it struck him- she didn't just need money, she needed courage and emotional support.

John began spending time with her every evening, listening, encouraging, and simply being present. His service was not financial anymore- it was emotional, steady, and full of love. His daughter slowly regained her confidence, and while the problems did not disappear instantly, she felt more confident to handle life.

Children are natural harbingers of change, of new ways of thinking and perspective. They challenge the mindset and behaviour, for example, they easily adapt to the new technology, language, or culture. It is the adult who instils fear, limitations, and archaic thinking, fixing the child in a box of stereotypes. This slows down the natural learning process.

The adult thinking they have more experience and, due to age as a stamp of seniority, believes that they know more. This is not to take the experience and learning away from the earlier generation; however, it is interesting to analyse that children keep the adult young, curious, informed, and childlike.

Parents are here to serve the children as guides or coaches. Bringing out the latent talents and powers. Not to superimpose or burden them with preconceived judgements, or archaic views. Every generation must be more progressive than the previous, not just in possessions, rather in mindset and vision. Some notable trends and studies highlight shifts in the mindset and priorities of the current generation. They are specifically rejecting alcohol consumption, materialism and prioritising work-life balance.

Studies have shown that millennials prefer spending money on experiences rather than possessions. An Eventbrite survey posted on Frontier Economics found that Britain's 18 to 34-year-olds are driving the experience economy, with 66% saying they feel more fulfilled by life experiences rather than buying a material item of the same value, and 62% planning to increase spending on experiences over possessions in the near future.

Most evidence points towards the fact that youngsters are focusing more on owning fewer items. With the advent of remote work, Gen Z spends a significant proportion of their income on travel and adventure, due to which longer stays and community living are on the rise. 'Quiet Quitting' is a trend where employees refuse to work and adhere to job descriptions. Companies offering wellness perks such as gym memberships, therapy sessions and flexible working hours are more attractive to younger employees.

Today's younger crowd is more understanding of the circular economy, and hence, start-ups focusing on sustainable health, environment and living are growing. ScienceDirect substantiates this phenomenon based on Gen Z's increasing willingness to engage in circular business models like product-as-a-service, take-back and repair. The article finds high readiness among Gen Z consumers in several sustainable contexts, reinforcing their role as early adopters of circular practices. Not only that, but this generation is also de-prioritising traditional milestones of marriage, while choosing growth and self-care through personal development courses, life coaching, or business coaching, etc. Relationships, health (physical and mental), work, choices, success, and community are being completely redefined.

As we can see in the case of Gen Z, children are the GPS navigators of progress in a real sense. While they are moving forward, parents and the older community need to offer a cushion, such that when they fall, they have the backing to get up and run again. At the same time, parents should not stop them from falling at all and overdo the protection bit. Over-protective parenting, referred to as 'Helicopter parenting', is where the parents shield their children from any kind of discomfort, failure, or struggle. Everything is provided, which leaves no hunger for the child to root for hampering the development of emotional resilience, compassion, and gratitude for what one has. There is a sense of entitlement before they hit the real world, and everything then looks like a challenge.

According to studies, children with overprotective parents show delayed academic and social development, low self-esteem, and are more likely to experience anxiety. UK's BioMed Central has conducted intensive empirical work on the subject, showing that overprotective parenting elevates social and academic anxiety (e.g., high school students in China), and frustrates basic psychological needs, which is associated with greater trait anxiety in adolescents. This is because, without exposure to real problems, risks, and failures, they struggle to build coping mechanisms. Researchers found that children who are constantly rescued by parents during tasks or handling conflicts give up more quickly when faced with challenges and expect external intervention, creating dependency.

Some cultures talk about the 'Failure to launch' phenomenon, where young adults stay dependent on their parents, and hence develop a fear of failure or lack of confidence. They believe they are incapable of handling situations on their own, and always need someone to help or rescue them- a phenomenon known as 'Learned helplessness'. There are some cultures that propose the 'Let them play and fall' philosophy, which helps children to adapt early in life. Some environments are generally harsh and aggressive, where children learn by experience.

That being said, it is natural and instinctual to safeguard children; however, too much protection as proof of love is detrimental. Constant intervention is not proof or validation of love, good parenting, or safety from guilt of not doing enough. Sometimes, parents could be projecting their own anxieties and fear of not being protected, or the struggles they went through that made them tough. This could also be amplified by societal judgements, and too much competition they went through and did not have the coping mechanisms.

In academic terms, 'No grades' and 'Everyone gets a certificate' lead to lower effort and motivation. When there is no hunger within you, stop striving harder. Deflating healthy competition glorifies comfort and mediocrity. Challenges then change are the only constant, and shutting our eyes, not being well prepared for it, is a state of marination for mental health issues.

Parents must also inculcate the right sense of competition in their children. The word competition originates from the Latin word "Competito", which derives from the word "Competere." Breaking it down- "Com" means together or with, and "Petere" means to strive, seek or aim for. Thus, the original sense of "Competere" was to strive together or seek something in common. It referred to individuals working toward a shared goal with a spirit of mutual striving rather than adversarial conflict. Over time, the meaning shifted to glorify rivalry, victory, recognition, or resources. Before we became the rats in the race to play at the hands of the industrial revolution, competition was all about pushing the envelope of human limits, something we cannot do alone.

For example, the evolution of 200m sprint timings is proof of human development, in 1979 Pietro Mennea set the record of 19.72 seconds, which stood for 17 years. Usain Bolt pushed the limits, achieving the current record of 19.19 seconds during the 2009 World Championships.

These improvements resulted from a collective effort of advancements in nutrition, training, equipment, technology, and biometrics. Human performance is not etched in stone or conceivable by humans. To serve the human purpose is to breach boundaries, by dreaming the impossible, questioning the status quo, breaking the old bonds of thinking; this is evident in the innovation and development in technology.

We need competition to exist in a supportive environment, where children are allowed to bring out their personal best as opposed to beating each other. The best performance should be seen as the potential of a human, rather than trying to beat the person. Service towards humanity is to bring out the best version of oneself and push the human potential. Setting challenging yet achievable goals from younger days, developing a growth mindset, pushing oneself out of a comfort zone by intentionally having perceived uncomfortable conversations, which promote self-awareness.

Kahlil Gibran's iconic poem "On Children" is an effective literary guide to how parents should view children. Gibran's words remind us that children are not the property of their parents; they are independent souls with a unique purpose and destiny.

"You may give them your love but not your thoughts, for they have their own thoughts. You may house their bodies but not their souls, for their souls dwell in the house of tomorrow, which you cannot visit, not even in your dreams."

– Kahlil Gibran

In the above verse, 'The house of tomorrow' is referred to as the higher souls of the children, which house their unique purpose and plan. Hence, they are not here to loan the fears, limitations, lacks and unfulfilled desires of their parents.

"You may strive to be like them, but seek not to make them like you. For life goes not backward nor tarries with yesterday."

– Kahlil Gibran

Gibran persuades us to be spontaneous, curious, childlike, and innovative while nurturing and guiding the children. The idea is to become flexible and not fixated, if we need to evolve.

They say, 'It takes a village to serve a child, and isn't that true? Children are seeds, and must be collectively nurtured by society for it to progress.

Beyond Obligation: Bonding With Elders

"My heroes are and were my parents. I can't see having anyone else as my heroes."

– Michael Jordan

Being a support for our parents is an unsaid law of giving back that honours the sacrifices, love, commitment they have poured in. In many Asian societies, caring for elderly parents is a moral, often religious or cultural duty.

In China, there exists a principle called 'Filial Piety', a concept emphasising respect and care for one's parents. Dating back to the pre-Confucian period and primitive ancestor worship practices, it is a fundamental virtue originating from ancient Chinese culture and Confucian philosophy, represented by the Chinese character 孝 (xiào), which consists of the character for "old" (老) above the character for "son" (子), symbolising an elder being supported by a child.

While children must support their parents on a physical and emotional level, both parties also need to acknowledge that excessive dependence leads to diminishing willpower. This may cause unwillingness to make independent efforts, too much comfort and a loss of autonomy on the parents' part. Such patterns eventually cause loss of mobility, memory loss, and acceleration of other physical and mental issues associated with old age. Willpower is essential for cognitive and physical functions of the body.

On the other hand, maintaining capabilities should not promote loneliness in the elderly. Western cultures glorify independence; hence, elderly parents live alone or in assisted living facilities. While this promotes self-reliance, it can lead to isolation and neglect if not balanced with active family balance.

A balanced approach is a way of service towards parents. How do we achieve a balanced approach? The plan is simple:

- **Volunteer work**- motivate parents to stay active through volunteer or community activities to give back their experience and wisdom to society
- **Quality time**- Spending meaningful time with parents gives them courage and reduces loneliness. Shared activities such as cooking pass on the family traditions, recipes, and culture. Parents draw energy from people around, especially young children.
- **Technology support**- Use innovative apps and gadgets to keep them monitored for physical health and connected to the modern world.

As adults lying in the middle of the passing generation and the coming generation, the most important service we can offer is working towards breaking old thought forms. Archaic, superstitious, fossilised beliefs persist until questioned and re-evaluated. These ideas limit the next generation and become a robotic ritual for the confused adult.

For the older generation, their perspectives on money, values, work, relationships, politics, gender roles, etc are part of the collective identity and culture. That may not be the case for the younger lot, and, as a result, they may not subscribe to vintage ideas of life and society. The generational disconnect has been created by these outdated beliefs, and change feels threatening when it challenges the beliefs that have guided decisions for decades. Here are some examples:

- Financial security is important in a good profession: Modern opportunities provide flexibility and security with the gig economy and entrepreneurship.
- Newly defined gender roles are fracturing relationships: Concepts of gender fluidity, shared responsibilities and diverse family structures are new.
- Hard work and physical labour are the only ways. Remote work is less real: Technology has transformed productivity and the value of intellectual and emotional labour.
- Community will progress by keeping the culture closed: Global cultures, diversity and inter-faith groups bring diversity and innovation.

Every system needs an upgrade, but unfortunately, unlike technology, for humans, the upgrade cannot be downloaded in a jiffy. Differentiating between beliefs rooted in values and those stemming from outdated and regressive systems requires a discerning approach. Here are a few ways one can discard beliefs which are detrimental to a growth mindset:

- Examine the purpose behind the existence of the belief:
  - **Values**: Beliefs rooted in growth, evolution, betterment, respect, compassion, and love have a universal, enduring, higher purpose

- **Superstition**: Beliefs that seem to keep knowledge with a few, serve to control the mind or behaviour, reinforce fear, uphold outdated hierarchies, lack logical or moral grounding (e.g., gender roles enforcing patriarchy, rituals based on fear or bad luck, etc)

- Assess the impact of the belief on the outcome:
  - **Growth-oriented**: Do these beliefs help individuals or communities grow?
  - **Regressive beliefs**: Which waste time, restrict individual freedom or perpetuate discrimination, may need some re-evaluation or tweaking.

- Relevance in the modern context:
  - **Values**: Some beliefs may be traditional, yet remain relevant in the modern context, e.g., be in gratitude, respect elders, and honesty is the best policy
  - **Archaic**: Some may no longer apply, e.g. women should stay at home to take care of the house and children. Respect is earned by age. Cannot argue or question someone in the hierarchy

The responsibility to take the community and thereby the country through development is achieved by gradually moving from regressive to progressive beliefs.

Paying It Forward, Where It Began

We are born in specific countries and cities for a reason; these are not mere coincidences, but carefully crafted alignments tied to the journey and purpose of our soul. The land we are born in is special; it carries the required essentials to bring out the potential in us. Plants can't grow without the nurturing environment of air, water, and sunlight.

We have a collective karma towards the nation by contributing to its progress, harmony, innovation, service, and peace. It is imperative to be good citizens as representatives of the land. At the same time, the nation offers us resources, culture, opportunities, and a sense of belonging. The collective energy of the nation is healthy pride.

To make a nation, one needs to participate in democracy by contributing to fair governance, standing up against injustices and questioning unethical practices. Focus on creating solutions for local communities, supporting the underserved areas and creating jobs through innovation, helping out during disasters, are various ways one can collectively uplift a nation. A sense of entitlement just because one pays taxes is a self-centred perspective. Taxes alone do not solve national problems; they are not dues to live in a country.

Only the contribution of the citizens can take a nation to progress, not politics or the economy. Historically, the objective of politics is to serve the people so that they can participate in the progress of the nation. Similarly, the law's purpose was to maintain order and protect the society's ethical fabric. Corruption and inefficiencies reflect the belly of the nation, its psyche towards 'Self- preservation vs nation building.' A nation inspires a vision through its people who take the responsibility of patriotism, a sense of collective ownership through innovation, ethical practices, and letting go of short-term gains for long-term peace.

Service is the living expression of gratitude, compassion and forgiveness- transforming these virtues from theoretical idea to tangible action. When we serve by acknowledging the blessings in our lives and sharing them with others, that is embodying gratitude. Self-healing happens when we transcend personal hurts, resentment, and grudges by helping those who may have wronged us. Service is the technique to forgive, forget, let go and create space for something expansive and alive. Compassion drives the intention of service, and not really the pride or pity to help someone below you. It is the energy which connects and wants to keep coming back to this feeling.

Service through faith

Service is the only path to be super powerful in a loving way, such that the efforts henceforth become easy with greater impact. That is most It is the foundation of most religions.

Selfless service in Sikhism is seen through 'Dasvandh', which translates to "tenth-part" where one-tenth of the income is or resources are contributed toward community welfare. The biggest example is the practice of 'Langar' (Serving Food) at every

Gurudwara. The practice embodies equality where everyone sits on the floor to eat food served by the community. The preparation of food, service and washing of the utensils is all managed by the volunteers.

A similar practice in Christianity is 'Tithing', where ten per cent of one's income is contributed towards charity, which is used for education, medical help, and other community development areas. Service through 'Zakat' is one of the five pillars of Islam, which again is a monetary contribution and is used to provide community service. The belief is that wealth is trust from Allah to be shared.

'Seva' or service in Hinduism is a path to spiritual growth. By giving, one aligns with the principle of 'Dharma'. It is also a way to purify oneself- it creates detachment from the concept of material wealth.

Service through initiative

The action within service unlocks the superpower of exponential growth. Create your own initiative that resonates with you. Meet the version of yourself that you haven't yet met.

The word service draws big, heroic projects- feeding an entire village, or starting a global movement. And while those are incredible feats, service at an individual level can be simple and surprisingly powerful. Service can be the new favourite currency, like spending time in a new café, hitting the gym or a new nutritional fad.

Service can be 'Social-Fitness'- create a group of volunteers to run together, plant trees, read books for the community children, mentor young adults and children, offer your skills to all age groups, such as technology skills to the old, soft skills to the young adults, and computer skills to children.

Service through conversations

Talking, listening, and creating safe spaces for people is also important, because most people don't need grand advice; they need to feel heard. Check in on people who matter. Ask real questions- What has been the hardest thing lately? What has given you the most joy? Do not be in a hurry to 'Fix' things, just stay. Creating safe spaces in relationships, personal or professional, is the most valued habit towards building trust. Presence in the moment without distraction is the biggest contribution.

Service through thoughts

This is an energetic contribution that is invisible, yet enormously powerful and one-pointed. Creating positive thoughts and blessings to the world, troubled areas, and people who need help. Blessings and positive intentions are silent, invisible ammunition that land at the target and create an enormously optimistic effect, especially where physically you cannot do much. The Twin Hearts Meditation is one such unique tool to bless the earth, people, and goals.

Turning daily actions into habits of service can make you emotionally and mentally abundant. Service is a revolution that dismantles hierarchies, disrupts the ego's monopoly, insisting that true fulfilment comes from interest, which involves self, harms no one and uplifts everyone. This is the superpower that will ensure humanity's relevance in a tech-driven world.

Technology cannot replicate emotions that is why with more connectivity comes loneliness and depression. Service is a new age skill set that will never be overtaken, go obsolete or irrelevant. Service is the magic humans embody.

Not Just Giving!

When you think of service, in a nutshell, all we can imagine is helping other people and other things. But what about us as receivers? As much as we should learn about giving service, we must also imbibe the art of receiving it with grace and dignity.

We all know that as a species, we humans are built a certain way, and it takes a lot of un-learning to iron out the chinks in our behaviour. One of these chinks is the absolute awkwardness and unwillingness to accept help, or accept it healthily. We may be more than happy to perform the act of service, but when it comes to embracing the service that comes our way, for some reason, it doesn't seem as smooth or easy.

Think of a friend who offers to help with carrying your bag during a holiday, or a colleague who does the same on a work trip. What's the first instinct that comes to mind? To refuse! To state that we can manage it. It's inbuilt in us. Even if we are lugging around more bags than we can, and lightening the load would really help, we generally don't like to accept help. This is how we function on a larger level, too. Give help? Yes. Take help? No.

Receiving service gracefully is also a pivotal part of the process. We should always know when to accept help and how to accept it. One must learn to say "yes" to help without feeling selfish, guilty, self-pity or agitation. This will not only lighten the many "loads" we carry mentally as well as physically, but also teach us to let go of ego when we actually need help.

Ultimately, it is this beautiful flow of giving and receiving that makes us who we are. Embracing service done for us is an important step in understanding how interwoven we are as a species, and even though we may survive in isolation, we thrive in a community built upon help and service.

Oprah Winfrey, the eponymous television host and philanthropist, famously said, "You can't do it all yourself. Don't be afraid to rely on others to help you accomplish your goals". This single quote says a thousand things about the power of accepting help and receiving service. The truth is, no one thrives alone.

It all begins with the first step, the first yes. The next time someone offers you a hand in any shape or form, right from a word of encouragement to even a listening ear, don't give in to your earlier instincts; pause refusing them. By receiving with grace, you are not taking; you are serving.

The Closing Note

In *Autobiography of a Yogi* by **Paramahansa Yogananda, the purpose of life, as taught by the rishis and ancient sages, is that each person is created by God as a soul to uniquely manifest a special attribute of the Infinite before resuming its absolute identity.**

When I wrote this book, my intention was simple: to remind you that what you are seeking outside has always been alive inside you. The four superpowers — **gratitude, compassion, forgiveness, and service** — are more than idealistic ideas. They are simple practices that can quietly transform how you think, feel and live. Secretly, these are interconnected with each other and come alive according to the level of development of the personality.

Think of them as daily vitamins to move ahead at a faster pace:

- **Gratitude** shifts your thoughts from scarcity to abundance, which naturally opens the door to better opportunities and prosperity.
- **Compassion** softens the way you relate to people. It reduces stress in your body and creates deeper, more genuine connections.
- **Forgiveness** frees you from the weight of old hurts, which improves your mental clarity, emotional health, and even your physical energy.

- **Service** lifts you out of self-centred worry and reminds you that you are part of something larger. It brings meaning, joy, and even a sense of good fortune.

You do not have to practice them perfectly or all at once. Begin small:

- Each morning, name one thing you are grateful for before reaching for anything.
- During the day, pause once to place yourself in someone else's shoes.
- In the evening, ask yourself if there is one memory or resentment you are ready to let go of.
- And once a day, offer a simple act of service — a smile, a message of encouragement, or a hand extended.

Now imagine yourself one year from today. If you practice these four superpowers consistently, you will not be the same person. You will notice that your friendships feel more meaningful. People will treat you with unexpected kindness. Random help will appear when you least expect it. Your days will carry less anxiety, and challenges will start to feel like healthy opportunities instead of heavy burdens. There will be more peace in your mind, and more flow in your life.

This is how you will know the superpowers are working: life itself will mirror back your inner change.

And the vision goes even further. Imagine what happens when these superpowers are not just practiced individually, but lived together as a community. A circle of people living their highest potential with these superpowers sends out a gentle resonance of trust, kindness, and support that touches everyone around them. Mistrust, fear and competition begin to dissolve, and a new sense of group consciousness takes root — where we lift each other, look out for one another, and grow side by side.

Wherever you are, each time you practice these qualities, you are adding to the energy of this planet. And as more of us choose to live this way, the idea strengthens. The spark becomes a flame and into a movement. This is the deeper vision: not just transforming yourself- becoming part of a collective force that makes the world gentler, wiser, and more whole.

Carry these practices with you. Share them with your friends. Gift the book, talk about it, invite others to join you. Together, we can build a world where gratitude, compassion, forgiveness, and service are not exceptions- A legacy we leave behind.

References

The First Super Power: Gratitude

The Unseen Gift

Etymology Online. (n.d.). Gratitude. Online Etymology Dictionary.
https://www.etymonline.com/word/gratitude

Yoga Journal. (n.d.). Anjali Mudra: Salutation Seal. Yoga Journal.
https://www.yogajournal.com/poses/anjali-mudra

Harvard Health Publishing. (2021). The science of gratitude. Harvard Medical School.
https://www.health.harvard.edu/mind-and-mood/the-science-of-gratitude

A Spiritual Perspective

Bringsoul.life (n.d.) Gratitude in Christianity
https://blog.bringsoul.life/posts/12_gratitude_in_christianity

Dr. Jaipal Singh. (n.d.). Gratitude in Hinduism.
https://www.boloji.com/articles/53698/hindu-hinduism-and-hindustan-part-lxxix

Quran 4:147. (n.d.). The Quranic Arabic Corpus.
https://corpus.quran.com/translation.jsp?chapter=4&verse=147

Smithsonian Institution. (n.d.). Harvest festivals around the world. Smithsonian.
https://www.si.edu/spotlight/harvest-festivals

Mahabharata. (n.d.). Story of Draupadi's pot and Krishna. Sacred Texts Archive.
https://www.sacred-texts.com/hin/maha/

Psalm 23:5, Holy Bible. Bible Gateway.
https://www.biblegateway.com/passage/?search=Psalm+23%3A5&version=NIV

Krishnamurti, J. (1983). On humility. Krishnamurti Foundation Trust.
https://jkrishnamurti.org/

When Control Misleads

Lao Tzu. (n.d.). Tao Te Ching. Taoist Texts Archive.
https://taoistic.com/

Kruger, J., & Dunning, D. (1999). Unskilled and unaware of it: How difficulties in recognizing one's own incompetence lead to inflated self-assessments. Journal of Personality and Social Psychology, 77(6), 1121–1134.
https://doi.org/10.1037/0022-3514.77.6.1121

Meadows, D. H. (2008). Thinking in systems: A primer. Chelsea Green Publishing.
https://virtualmmx.ddns.net/gbooks/ThinkinginSystems.pdf

Medical News Today. (n.d.). Tall poppy syndrome.
https://www.medicalnewstoday.com/articles/tall-poppy-syndrome
Maslow, A. H. (1943). A theory of human motivation. Psychological Review, 50(4), 370–396.
https://psychclassics.yorku.ca/Maslow/motivation.htm

Kaleidoscope of Kingdoms

Powell, A. E. (1930). The solar system. The Theosophical Publishing House.
https://www.anandgholap.net/Solar_System-AP.htm
Wikipedia contributors. (n.d.). Law of cause and effect (karma). In Wikipedia.
https://en.wikipedia.org/wiki/Karma
Lao Tzu. (n.d.). Tao Te Ching. Taoist Texts Archive.
https://taoistic.com/
Greater Good Science Center. (2015). How gratitude promotes humility. UC Berkeley.
https://greatergood.berkeley.edu/article/item/how_gratitude_promotes_humility
Maslow, A. H. (1954). Motivation and personality. Harper & Row.

The Kauravas Within Us

Vyasa. (n.d.). Mahabharata: The story of Arjuna and Duryodhana with Krishna. Sacred Texts Archive.
https://www.sacred-texts.com/hin/maha/
Yogananda, P. (1946). Self-realization teachings. Self-Realization Fellowship.
https://www.ananda.org/autobiography/
Krishnamurti, J. (1983). On psychological revolution. Krishnamurti Foundation Trust.
https://jkrishnamurti.org/

Authenticity Over Approval

Boyraz et al., 2014; Kim et al., 2023; Ostermeier et al., 2022; Song et al., 2021; Thomaes et al., 2017; Wickham et al., 2016; Wood et al., 2008; Xia et al., 2022). In addition, authentic individuals also report lower levels of psychological distress, aggressive behaviour, interpersonal conflict, job burnout, and turnover intention (Bryan et al., 2017; Ostermeier et al., 2022; Pinto et al., 2012; Song et al., 2021; Theran, 2011; Tou et al., 2015
Socrates. (n.d.). Know thyself. The Internet Classics Archive.
http://classics.mit.edu/Plato/apology.html
Reese Y.W. Tou, Zachary G. Baker, Benjamin W. Hadden, Yi-Cheng Lin (2015 November) The real me: Authenticity, interpersonal goals, and conflict tactics.
https://www.sciencedirect.com/science/article/abs/pii/S0191886915003724
Chad E. Lakey, Michael H. Kernis, Whitney L. Heppner, Charles E. Lance. Individual differences in authenticity and mindfulness as predictors of verbal defensiveness.
https://www.sciencedirect.com/science/article/abs/pii/S0092656607000645
Orly Shapira-Lishchinsky and Sigalit Tsemach (2014 January 8). Psychological Empowerment as a Mediator Between Teachers' Perceptions of Authentic Leadership and Their Withdrawal and Citizenship Behaviors

https://journals.sagepub.com/doi/10.1177/0013161X13513898
C. R. Snyder, Shane J. Lopez (2005). Handbook of positive psychology.
https://archive.org/details/handbookofpositi0000unse_b8m7/page/n3/mode/2up
Güler Boyraz, J Brandon Waits, Victoria A Felix (2014 July). Authenticity, life satisfaction, and distress: a longitudinal analysis.
https://pubmed.ncbi.nlm.nih.gov/25019552/
Boyraz, G., Waits, J. B., & Felix, V. A. (2014). Authenticity, life satisfaction, and distress: A longitudinal analysis. Journal of Counseling Psychology, 61(3), 498–505.
https://ouci.dntb.gov.ua/en/works/9Jo6D5E7/
Kim, T. Y. (2023). Authenticity or self-enhancement? Effects of trust from coworkers on job performance via authentic self-expression. Personality and Social Psychology Bulletin.
https://journals.sagepub.com/doi/full/10.1177/01492063211063807
Ostermeier, M., et al. (2022). [Study on authenticity benefits].
https://www.researchgate.net/figure/Descriptive-statistics-and-correlations-study-2_tbl2_361616752
Wood, A. M., Linley, P. A., Maltby, J., Baliousis, M., & Joseph, S. (2008). The authentic personality: A theoretical and empirical conceptualization and the development of the Authenticity Scale. Journal of Counseling Psychology.
https://www.researchgate.net/publication/362042968_Authenticity_Meaning_in_Life_and_Life_Satisfaction_A_Multicomponent_Investigation_of_Relationships_at_the_Trait_and_State_Levels

The Science of Waiting

Mischel, W., Shoda, Y., & Rodriguez, M. I. (1989). Delay of gratification in children. Science, 244(4907), 933–938.
https://doi.org/10.1126/science.2658056
National Institute of Mental Health. (n.d.). Prefrontal cortex and executive function. NIMH.
https://www.nimh.nih.gov/
Frankl, V. E. (1946). Man's search for meaning. Beacon Press.

Wired For Wonder

Cleveland Clinic. (n.d.). Fight-or-flight response: Definition, hormones, and impact. Cleveland Clinic.
https://my.clevelandclinic.org/health/articles/21271-fight-or-flight-response
Mayo Clinic. (2022). Stress symptoms: Effects on your body and behavior. Mayo Clinic.
https://www.mayoclinic.org/healthy-lifestyle/stress-management/in-depth/stress-symptoms/art-20050987
APA. (n.d.). Gratitude and health: The link explained. American Psychological Association.
https://www.apa.org/news/press/releases/stress/2011/gratitude-health
Harari, M. B., Reaves, A. C., & Viswesvaran, C. (2016). Job satisfaction and job performance: A meta-analysis. Journal of Applied Psychology, 101(9), 1332–1350.
https://doi.org/10.1037/apl0000128

You Can Move Mountains!

Greater Good Science Center. (n.d.). How to keep a gratitude journal. UC Berkeley.
https://greatergood.berkeley.edu/article/item/how_to_keep_a_gratitude_journal

Seligman, M. E. P., Steen, T. A., Park, N., & Peterson, C. (2005). Positive psychology progress: Empirical validation of interventions. American Psychologist, 60(5), 410–421.
https://doi.org/10.1037/0003-066X.60.5.410

The Second Super Power: Compassion

Lead with the Heart

Darwin, C. (1859). On the origin of species. John Murray.
https://www.gutenberg.org/ebooks/1228

Spencer, H. (1864). Principles of biology. Williams and Norgate.
https://archive.org/details/principlesofbiol01spenuoft

Cleveland Clinic. (n.d.). Fight-or-flight response: Definition, hormones, and impact. Cleveland Clinic.
https://my.clevelandclinic.org/health/articles/21271-fight-or-flight-response

Buddha & The Real Kingdom

Narada Thera. (1998). The Buddha and his teachings. Buddhist Publication Society.
https://www.bps.lk/olib/bp/bp503s_Narada_Buddha-and-His-Teachings.pdf

Paramahansa Yogananda. (1946). Autobiography of a yogi. Self-Realization Fellowship.
https://www.ananda.org/autobiography/

Encyclopedia Britannica. (n.d.). Gautama Buddha.
https://www.britannica.com/biography/Buddha-founder-of-Buddhism

Tibetan Buddhist Encyclopedia. (n.d.). Angulimala.
https://tibetanbuddhistencyclopedia.com/en/index.php/Buddhist_Story:_Angulimala:_A_Story_of_the_Power_of_Compassion

Plato. (n.d.). Allegory of the cave. In The Republic. MIT Classics Archive.
http://classics.mit.edu/Plato/republic.html

The Allegory of the Cave

Harvard Scholar. (n.d.). Allegory of the cave.
https://scholar.harvard.edu/files/seyer/files/plato_republic_514b-518d_allegory-of-the-cave.pdf

Bhagavad Gita. (n.d.). Chapter 2, Verse 47 (Nishkam Karma). Sacred Texts Archive.
https://www.sacred-texts.com/hin/gita/bg02.htm

Tao Te Ching. (n.d.). Wu Wei philosophy. Taoist Texts Archive.
https://taoistic.com/

Csikszentmihalyi, M. (1990). Flow: The psychology of optimal experience. Harper & Row.
https://www.researchgate.net/publication/224927532_Flow_The_Psychology_of_Optimal_Experience

Epictetus. (n.d.). Stoic teachings on detachment. Internet Classics Archive.

http://classics.mit.edu/Epictetus/epicench.html

The Inner Compass

Golnaz Tabibnia, Matthew D Lieberman, Michelle G Craske. The Lasting Effect of Words on Feelings: Words May Facilitate Exposure Effects to Threatening Images.
https://pmc.ncbi.nlm.nih.gov/articles/PMC4727455/
Positive Reinforcement Mediated by Midbrain Dopamine Neurons.
https://pmc.ncbi.nlm.nih.gov/articles/PMC3986242/
Quantum and Electromagnetic Fields in Our Universe and Brain- A New Perspective to Comprehend Brain Function
https://www.psychologicalscience.org/
Matt Tenney. People Thriver (n.d). Employee Motivation and Its Impact on Productivity.
https://peoplethriver.com/employee-motivation-and-its-impact-on-productivity/
Yeseul Jung, Young Woo Sohn. Does work passion benefit or hinder employee's career commitment? (2022 Jun 3)
https://pmc.ncbi.nlm.nih.gov/articles/PMC9165830/
Erin J. Wamsley. Dreaming, waking conscious experience, and the resting brain.
https://www.frontiersin.org/journals/psychology/articles/10.3389/fpsyg.2013.00637/full
Karun Meda. The Heart's "Little Brain". Jefferson.edu (2022 April 19)
https://research.jefferson.edu/2022-magazine/the-hearts-little-brain.html
Rollin McCraty, Mike Atkinson, Raymond Trevor Bradley. Electrophysiological evidence of intuition. (2004 Feb)
https://pubmed.ncbi.nlm.nih.gov/15025887/
How Self-Appraisal Is Mediated by the Brain. Frontiersin.org (2021 June 29)
https://www.frontiersin.org/journals/human-neuroscience/articles/10.3389/fnhum.2021.700046/full
Self Compassion (n.d). Dr. Kristin Neff.
https://self-compassion.org/the-research/
Get to Know the 8 Limbs of Yoga (n.d). Yoga Journal.
https://www.yogajournal.com/yoga-101/philosophy/8-limbs-of-yoga/eight-limbs-of-yoga/
Todoist (n.d.). The Pomodoro Technique.
https://www.todoist.com/productivity-methods/pomodoro-technique

The Third Super Power: Forgiveness

The Paradox we live with

Bartlett, C. (2024, November 14). How social media is reshaping human connection. 360info.
https://360info.org/how-social-media-is-reshaping-human-connection/
Dovan, C. (2024, August 23). What to know about the hive mind mentality. Verywell Mind.
https://www.verywellmind.com/hive-mind-mentality-8697047

The Many faces of our emotions

Equanima. (n.d.). Only 4% of people can name what they're feeling and it affects mental health.
https://equanima.io/only-of-people-can-name-what-they-feeling/
Plutchik's Wheel of Emotions: Exploring the Feelings Wheel and How to Use It (n.d.)
https://www.6seconds.org/2025/02/06/plutchik-wheel-emotions
Dr. Gloria Wilcox. The Feeling Wheel (1982).
https://thefeelingswheel.com/wp-content/uploads/2024/09/willcox1982_feelingswheel.pdf
The Neuroscience of Growth Mindset & Intrinsic Motivation. Betsy Ng. (2018 Jan 26)
https://pmc.ncbi.nlm.nih.gov/articles/PMC5836039/
Yohanes Budiarto, Avin Fadilla Helmi. Shame and Self-Esteem: A Meta-Analysis.
https://pmc.ncbi.nlm.nih.gov/articles/PMC4040090/

Opposites Don't just attract

Mindfulness and emotion regulation—an fMRI study (2013 May 29)
https://pmc.ncbi.nlm.nih.gov/articles/PMC4040090/
Three Initiates. (1908). The Kybalion: A study of the Hermetic philosophy of Ancient Egypt and Greece. Yogi Publication Society.
https://www.yogebooks.com/english/atkinson/1908kybalion.pdf
Solgood Media. (n.d.). The Kybalion: 7 Hermetic principles explained in simple terms. Solgood Media.
https://solgoodmedia.com/blog/the-kybalion-7-hermetic-principles-explained-in-simple-terms

The Perfect frequency

Alice Bailey (n.d.). The science of the seven rays.
https://www.lucistrust.org/arcane_school/talks_and_articles/the_science_the_seven_rays

Finding inner strength

Loren L Toussaint, Grant S Shields, George M Slavich. Forgiveness, Stress, and Health: a 5-Week Dynamic Parallel Process Study.
https://pmc.ncbi.nlm.nih.gov/articles/PMC5055412/
Meditation on Twin Hearts. (n.d.). Meditation on twin hearts.
https://meditationontwinhearts.com/
Trafton, A. (2025, January 15). How one brain circuit encodes memories of both places and events. MIT News.
https://news.mit.edu/2025/how-one-brain-circuit-encodes-memories-places-and-events-0115
Yuval Nir. Giulio Tononi. (2010 Jan 14) Dreaming and the brain: from phenomenology to neurophysiology.
https://pmc.ncbi.nlm.nih.gov/articles/PMC2814941/
Anne Trafton (2025 Jan 15). How one brain circuit encodes memories of both places and events. MIT News.
https://news.mit.edu/2025/how-one-brain-circuit-encodes-memories-places-and-events-0115

Forgiveness and death

P van Lommel, R van Wees, V Meyers, I Elfferich (2001 December 15). Near-death experience in survivors of cardiac arrest.
https://pubmed.ncbi.nlm.nih.gov/11755611/
Dannion Brinkley (1994). Saved by the Light: The True Story of a Man Who Died Twice and the Profound Revelations He Received.
Anita Moorjani (2012). Dying to be Me.
Dr. Eben Alexander (2012). Proof of Heaven: A Neurosurgeon's Journey into the Afterlife.
Svenja Brodt, Marion Inostroza, Niels Niethard, Jan Born (2023 April 5). Sleep—A brain-state serving systems memory consolidation.
https://www.sciencedirect.com/science/article/pii/S0896627323002015

The Fourth Super Power: Service

Living On Purpose

Shams-E-Tabrizi. (n.d.). Quotation on divine spirit and human responsibility. [Primary Source].
Suzanne W. Simard, David A. Perry, Melanie D. Jones, David D. Myrold, Daniel M. Durall & Randy Molina (1997 August 7). Net transfer of carbon between ectomycorrhizal tree species in the field.
https://www.nature.com/articles/41557
Frontiers in Psychology. (2023). The interpersonal costs of phubbing and problematic smartphone usage. Frontiers.
https://www.frontiersin.org/articles/10.3389/fpsyt.2023.1123456/full
BMJ. (2023). Problematic levels of loneliness: A systematic review across 113 countries. The BMJ.
https://www.bmj.com/content/382/bmj-2023-072893
Ernst & Young. (2025). Growing user fatigue with AI: The rise of preference for human experience. EY Global.
https://www.ey.com/en_gl/insights/ai/growing-user-fatigue-ai
Three Initiates. (1912). The Kybalion: Chapter XII. Causation. Sacred-Texts.com.
https://sacred-texts.com/eso/kyb/kyb14.htm
Duangjina, T., Jeamjitvibool, T., & Park, C. (2025). Sex and gender differences in caregiver burden among family caregivers of persons with dementia: A systematic review and meta-analysis. Archives of Gerontology and Geriatrics, 138, 105977.
https://www.sciencedirect.com/science/article/pii/S0167494325002341
de Graaff, M. L. A., van der Heide, I., Rademakers, J. J. D. J. M., van Valkengoed, I. G. M., Francke, A. L., Woonink, A., & Bijnsdorp, F. M. (2025, March 14). Is caregiver burden associated with sex and gender-related characteristics? A large-scale survey study among family caregivers of people with dementia. BMC Geriatrics, 25(1), 171.
https://doi.org/10.1186/s12877-025-05795-y

Singh, P. P. (2025, July 10). Emotional Suppression and Depression in Indian Men. The Academic: International Journal of Multidisciplinary Research. https://doi.org/10.5281/zenodo.15866307

Balance Before Burnout

PubMed Central. (n.d.). Caregiver burden and quality of life: Health impacts of caregiving. National Center for Biotechnology Information.
https://pmc.ncbi.nlm.nih.gov/articles/PMC1122334/
Powell, A. E. (1928). The causal body and the ego. The Theosophical Publishing House.
https://www.anandgholap.net/Causal_Body_And_The_Ego-AP.htm
Bailey, A. A. (1934). A treatise on white magic. Lucis Trust.
https://www.lucistrust.org/store/item/white_magic

More Than Mere Duty

Yogananda, P. (n.d.) Chapter 12: Years in My Master's Hermitage. In Autobiography of a Yogi (Crystal Clarity Publishers).
https://www.crystalclarity.com/en-in/pages/autobiography-chapter-12-years-in-my-masters-hermitage
Greenleaf, R. K. (1970). The servant as leader. Greenleaf Center for Servant Leadership.
https://www.greenleaf.org/what-is-servant-leadership/

Raising, Not Owning

Eventbrite. (2014). Millennials fuel the experience economy. Eventbrite & Frontier Economics.
https://eventbrite.co.uk/blog/academy/millennials-experience-economy/
ScienceDirect. (2023). Gen Z and circular economy adoption: A systematic review. Elsevier.
https://www.sciencedirect.com/science/article/pii/S095965262300XXX
BioMed Central. (2022). Overprotective parenting and adolescent anxiety: A cross-cultural study. BMC Psychology. https://bmcpsychology.biomedcentral.com/articles/10.1186/s40359-022-00789-0

Beyond Obligation: Bonding With Elders

Confucius. (n.d.). The concept of filial piety (孝). Confucian classics archive. xiao (孝).
https://en.wikipedia.org/wiki/Filial_piety
World Health Organization. (2022). Social isolation and loneliness among older people.
https://www.who.int/news-room/fact-sheets/detail/social-isolation-and-loneliness